A Manual

for a

Contemporary

Body

Ivana Daniell

Published by That Guy's House

www.thatguyshouse.com

IVANA DANIELL
ID

To my sons Vinci and Christian.

The lights of my life!

Acknowledgments

A very big thank you to the amazing people who have made my dream come true, to finally publish my book.

To my wonderful editor Deborah Murrell, I would have not made it without you.

To the very talented Jenni Woodhead, my book designer, and to Emanuela Fociani, my illustrator, you were a pleasure to work with.

To my publisher, Sean Patrick, of That Guy's House.

To my neuroscientist friend Julia Bornemann, who taught me all about the brain.

To my dear superman AY, we have spent over a decade exploring the infinite potential of the human body. Your dedication to my work sets an example to those who are searching for a more intelligent and healthier way of moving.

And finally, to all of you, my wonderful clients and friends who have inspired me and supported me across the arc of my career.

Contents

Introduction

There is nothing more appealing than a healthy, fit and posture-confident BODY. No matter what SIZE or AGE, the confidence that a person exudes is the real secret and passport to an ageless and youthful life.

Since I was a child my main life motivator has been movement. As a little girl, I discovered the joy of dancing; I started ballet when I was four years old. From dancing, I moved to study the human body. Today I run my own practice where I teach people to reconnect and understand this amazing creation called the human body. The choices I made as a young woman gave me the opportunity to travel around the world, discovering new countries and new cultures, moving further and further from the career my parents had chosen for me, towards a different destiny. It has been an incredible journey and a true gift to be able to follow my passion. This has kept me young at heart, and young in mind and body. The same passion now drives me to share my experience and guide others to discover how they too can capture, maintain or recapture the vitality and joy of an **ageless body.** It is also my mission in life to point those who seek **a healthier lifestyle** in the right direction and guide them through the choices that will give them complete control of their bodies and destinies. Enjoy!

PROUD TO TELL MY AGE

My name is Ivana; I am in my 60s and proud to tell the world my age.

I once thought twice about revealing my age to the world, but today I do it with great pride. Although I have already passed the so-called "middle

9

age", today, in my 60s, I feel at the pinnacle of my life. I look and feel healthier, stronger, younger, and more confident than I ever felt before. For me, life began a new and exciting cycle at 50!

I have the gift of the wisdom and experience of a mature woman, two beautiful grown-up sons, a beautiful grandchild, a fulfilling career, and a strong, fit, and healthy BODY. I realize that my chronological age no longer matches the way I feel about myself. I feel and think young!

People keep asking me what my secret is. How is it possible that I am so active and energetic, that I look and feel younger than I did 20 years ago? For many years my family, patients and friends have asked me to share "my secret" and now I am ready to do it with you, readers.

WE NEED TO MOVE!

Our body has been designed to be in movement. A body that does not move is dysfunctional, and like a machine that is not used it will get rusty and eventually break down. A healthy body, free from pain and capable of enjoying the freedom of movement will give you a sense of general well-being. This wonderful natural "high", accompanied by that positive feeling, is the most powerful anti-ageing and anti-depressant combination, a truly natural life motivator.

This positive attitude, this connection with your body that you will redis-cover through healthy and intelligent movement, is the first link of the chain that will anchor you to a future of health and vigour for the rest of your life.

WHAT IS A CONTEMPORARY BODY?

It is a body that is facing the challenges and advantages of today's contemporary lifestyle.

The main challenge our body is facing in our contemporary society is a more sedentary lifestyle. Since the beginning of our existence, our body was meant to be in movement, but, especially during the past 50 years, with technology growing so fast, we have lost the connection with our primary tool, our incredible vehicle; our body.

The main advantage of our contemporary lifestyle is that our lifespan has greatly extended. We have ahead of us a few more decades than we ever had before, and we need to make the best of them. In a society where the 50s are the new 30s, it is mandatory; if we make the best use of those decades ahead of us, our 80s could become the new 60s.

How can you achieve an ageless body?

First of all, take responsibility for your vehicle and learn how to drive it like a skilled Formula 1 driver. This precious vehicle is your best companion, and if you take proper care, it will not let you down during the ride of your life.

How do *we* or *you* do it?

- *Start by developing a better Body Awareness.*

- *Understand your Body Identity and your unique perfectly engineered vehicle.*

- *Exercise regularly and create correct movement patterns and healthy habits to support a strong body, free from pain.*

- *Start making informed and intelligent choices when choosing your activities and exercise programmes.*

- *Improve your working environment and make it posturally functional.*

- *Learn to go through a midlife challenge such as menopause with the correct information and a positive attitude. Look at it as the beginning of a new and exciting phase of your life!*

- *Rediscover the most important activity of your body, breathing.*

My ultimate aim is to give you an easy-to-follow manual with the necessary tools to improve your lifestyle, and achieve an AGELESS BODY.

THE CHALLENGES

- *Is it possible to stop or reverse the ageing clock?*
- *Is it possible to maintain a healthy, youthful body throughout our life, and enjoy the pleasures of a prolonged youth?*
- *Is it possible to minimize the damages of sagging muscles and skin due to the unavoidable effect of gravity?*

Yes, it is indeed possible, and obtainable by anyone.

There is no secret; I have simply applied one basic rule: I have never stopped being very active and exercising regularly and intelligently.

You are probably thinking, so what... please, I have heard this one before! There is nothing new about this. I have been exercising too. I have sweated for years with no great results. I don't feel any younger. My clock is still ticking my life away. My body is aching, and gravity is taking over!

But wait a minute, I am not finished; there is more... You may ask now, what have I done so differently to obtain such great results first with my own body and then with so many of my clients who have enjoyed the benefits of my BODY ID Method? Here is my answer:

I have taken a very different perspective when thinking about physical activities and exercise programmes. I strongly believe that the old equation often applied to physical exercise, NO PAIN, NO GAIN, no longer applies to today's Contemporary Body and people's lifestyles.

The 80s of the aerobic craze are long-gone; even the beautiful Jane Fonda, my ultimate idol, is today following a different, more gentle and contemporary exercise regime, and at 83 she rocks!

The 90s and the gym craze no longer apply to today's lifestyle, because we are moving towards a different body consciousness, a new era where people are searching for different body awareness.

It's the time for a new manual and for a new body, a Contemporary Body.

The old approach of breaking your body to be fit is outdated. A personal trainer who tells you there are no results without pain is simply propagating a myth.

Unfortunately, many people go to the gym or decide to go running without any movement, postural preparation, education or awareness. They do not have the correct information about what kind of exercise would be most suited to their personal needs. Often the choice is more dictated by **the body's appearance rather than the body's efficiency.**

My BODY ID approach is definitely the opposite; my followers and I go with the motto: NO PAIN, YES GAIN. We choose a very intelligent and scientific approach that respects the principles of biomechanics. A very organic approach that respects and heals the body instead of damaging it.

A SUSTAINABLE BODY

It all starts from being aware of this beautiful vehicle we have been given to ride during the journey of our life, 'The Human Body', learning to understand it and drive it correctly, just as you would a beautiful car.

If the physical body is in good postural alignment, it will move efficiently, therefore it will allow you to perform your daily tasks freely and enjoy your favourite activities and sports. As a bonus, this natural muscle connection will result in a very harmonious body shape. **A healthy, beautifully shaped body is a result of a mechanically efficient body.**

THE SOLUTION

BODY ID: My method

Based on many years of professional experience in Dance, Intelligent Movement Methods, Movement Therapy, and studies of the human body, having also personally dealt with a bad back injury, and finally having worked with so many different bodies and injuries, and heard so many interesting stories, I offer a unique approach to health and exercise programmes. **I believe in customizing movement/exercise routines for each individual, depending on their very personal needs and on their BODY ID.**

OUR BODY is UNIQUE; it is different from anyone else's.

When creating a programme I take into consideration many different aspects, such as:

- *The person's lifestyle, including the work environment.*

- *The person's movement personality.*

- *The person's body type.*

- *The person's posture and their genetic imprint.*

- *The person's clinical history.*

I also study and observe, if any, the current exercise regimes that the person is following and suggest appropriate modifications.

This is your BODY IDENTITY.

I strongly believe that before you start your journey to transformation, it is necessary to understand your body and, most important of all, to reconnect with it.

YOUR BODY HAS A STORY; it is written in your movements, in your muscles, in your posture, in every inch of your body; you just need to learn how to read it. What you are today is simply the result of years of habits, of a chosen lifestyle or, sadly, the result of an illness or an injury.

YOUR BODY IS INTELLIGENT; it adapts to different environments and different habits. Depending on your lifestyle it will deteriorate, or it will heal and improve.

The simple truth is, **your body can change,** at any time of your journey.

Though you may feel today that your vehicle is getting rusty, or you have lost the capacity to move your body efficiently because you have lost that natural connection, that muscle intelligence can be reinstalled, it is in your default system.

Remember that every single organ, every cell in our body has a perfect role to play, and all our muscles and bones are meant to be used and moved in unison.

In our contemporary society where life expectancy has doubled, when the 50s are the new 30s, when the pressure to achieve a more youthful appearance is even more evident, why can't we enjoy the extended pleasure of a strong, fit and healthy body at any age?

My Manual

I have written this manual for YOU, men and women, who have been searching for better life quality, who want to enjoy a beautiful, strong and efficient body until the end of the journey. Men and women who have been juggling careers with family obligations and at the same time struggling with a busy and a less physically active lifestyle. In particular, I have focused on those who suffer from the aches and pains that plague our sedentary contemporary society, who have tried everything, but for whom nothing has worked.

It is my sincere belief that through this manual I can help everyone to shorten their journey through the jungle of information and misinformation, to achieve a healthier body and a well-balanced, active and healthy life, to learn how to exercise in a more functional and intelligent manner, without the risk of injuries. I can help you to get the very best out of your chosen sport and favourite leisure activity. In addition, and most importantly, it will enable you simply to move functionally and easily during the course of your daily activities.

How will you benefit from reading my manual?

As a Movement and Posture expert, it is my mission to educate and guide people to make the right choices when concerning their bodies and when choosing specific activities or exercise programmes.

In my manual I will:

1.   *Provide you with my expertise; I will share in a simple, concise and practical way what has taken me years of studies and observation of the human body to learn. I will also share with you touching, life-changing stories that illustrate the healing power of movement.*

2.   *Teach you how to gain a better understanding of your own BODY ID;*

     - Your posture,

     - Your body type,

     - Your movement personality, and

     - What kinds of exercise programmes are most suited for you.

3.   *Explain the importance of maintaining a good posture, how to maintain strong core support and, finally, the importance of correct breathing with some practical awareness exercises.*

4. *__Inform__ you about the Intelligent Movement methods available today and how to access them.*

5. *__Guide__ you on how to choose the right exercise regime best suited to your specific needs.*

A truly up-to-date, modern and current Manual for a Contemporary Body.

Kindly note that **this is not an exercise book:** Exercise has to be done in the proper environment and with the appropriate professional guidance. Instead, I will give simple and useful information that you will be able to apply in your daily life, and some simple, easy activities, or movement awareness exercises, which you can practise at home or at work and use to rediscover your body. Your newfound body awareness will enable you then to make better and more conscious choices for your body, your fitness and, finally, your future health.

CHAPTER 1

FROM PAIN TO GAIN:
My Injury Story

When I was in my late 20s and at the peak of my dancing career, I suffered my first serious dance injury. I was pirouetting during a dance rehearsal in a dance studio in Italy. I lost my balance, fell, and broke my foot. I was in a cast for several weeks. Nothing could have been worse; I was facing the ultimate dancer's nightmare. Not being able to dance!

As soon as the cast was removed, I was immediately up on my toes, or rather, up on the tips of my toes, pirouetting and dancing as if nothing had happened. I was not advised by the doctor to do any particular post-rehabilitation exercises to strengthen the weakened leg, so I went straight back to dancing.

It was right after this first accident that I started to suffer from persistent lower back pain. I was young; I felt strong and invincible. I didn't pay any attention to the pain I was experiencing. I ignored these warning signs which, a few years later, resolved into a painful and chronic lower back condition that made me more vulnerable to further serious injury.

A few years later, in Paris, after the birth of my first son, Vinci, while performing a light and graceful "grand jeté" (a big jump in the air), I fell and landed heavily on my rear. The pain was incredibly intense, but with the determination typical of a dancer I got up and continued my dance rehearsal. I had no choice, really. I didn't want to lose my job and the opportunity to dance in the most important performance of my career, a big gala night at the Théâtre des Champs-Elysées, featuring the biggest international ballet stars. It was my dream! The morning after, when I woke up, I could hardly move. The pain in my lower back was excruciating. I was bewildered. Nothing had been broken, I was sure. I had been able to get up after my fall, very sore and limping, but still, I had been able to continue with the rehearsal.

I was stuck in bed for a few days. The doctor reassured me nothing had been broken, gave me the usual painkillers, and told me to rest.

All too soon I was back at work, where I was teaching dance, and at the same time rehearsing for the big show. I struggled with the remorseless pain as I continued my pirouetting. I had no choice if I wanted to perform in the great ballet gala show.

I spent the next couple of months in constant pain. I spent my spare time and what little money I had visiting osteopaths, acupuncturists, massage therapists, and any practitioner recommended to me. Nothing and no one could relieve my pain.

Finally, the much-awaited Gala Show at the Théâtre des Champs-Elysées arrived. The pain was as persistent as ever. During the show, a colleague noticed my discomfort and suggested that I apply some of his magic cream to numb the unbearable pain. No one thought to mention that the "magic cream" was a hot chilli-based cream to rub into the muscles to warm them up to a point where the intense heat would ease the pain. Dutifully, and with gratitude to a helpful colleague, in the rush of a costume change, I rubbed the magic chilli cream into the area of pain... my lower back... my very lower back... You can imagine the effect of the chilli cream in my rear... It was fire... chilli hot, in fact! I jumped and leapt through the air with seeming effortlessness. The show was a resounding success. I had survived the chilli treatment and given a hot performance on the stage.

That night after the show, after the ridiculous incident of the chilli cream, I decided I could no longer continue like this. The following day I went to the hospital to see an orthopaedic doctor. After a thorough examination and an x-ray, I was told I had a herniated disc[1] in my lumbar spine. I was advised to rest and be very careful. How can you tell this to a dancer whose life is all about movement?

---

1 A herniated disc is when that little soft cushion of tissue between the bones in your spine, the vertebrae, is pushed out of place.

I stopped performing and concentrated on my teaching career. I was devastated.

Months passed, but my pain seemed to be getting worse rather than better. Now my left leg was constantly hurting, because of my sciatica pain.[2]

The pain was always there, some days worse, some days better. But, like many people with chronic pain, I had learned to live with it.

I lived like this for years. I continued with my dance classes, my teaching career, and my studies. I continued to visit osteopaths, chiropractors and acupuncturists. They provided temporary relief that lasted a day or two if I was lucky. I could no longer carry my groceries. I had to be careful when carrying my children, and I had to be extra careful when taking my ballet classes. Basically, I had to be careful with everything. I had lost the freedom and the joy of movement. My back pain was controlling my life and I had no choice but to accept it. Then I reached the point when I could no longer enjoy my favourite activities.

Now living in London, I sought the advice of another orthopaedic doctor, who recommended an operation on my knees as a part of the solution to my problem. I was often unable to go for even short walks, as my knees would suddenly stop supporting me. However, the thought of having my knees cut open did not appeal to me in the least.

I had reached rock bottom. I was depressed and despairing. It was at this point that my wonderful ballet teacher, who had suffered a whiplash injury, suggested that I try an exercise method called Pilates, which had helped her in the recovery from her injury.

---

2 Sciatica pain is caused by an irritated nerve, the sciatic nerve. It's normally felt from the bottom down to the legs and in severe cases to your feet and toes. As in my case, it is commonly caused by a slipped or herniated disc in the lower spine.

I was willing to try anything at this point to avoid an operation.

I decided there and then to at least have a look at the Pilates studio above my ballet school.

This was in the late 80s, and the name PILATES could not be used owing to a legal issue involving the trademark, so studios used alternative names, and they were not listed under this discipline. This made them almost impossible to find. Pilates' studios were recommended mainly by word of mouth. They were almost exclusively known only to elite movers, such as dancers and sports professionals, who, like me, were suffering from an injury. Some actors and singers also attended these studios to improve their posture and deportment.

It was the dawn of Pilates and only a few people, who we call now first generation Pilates, were teaching it, a handful in all the world. I was very lucky to be part of the dawn of this amazing method and learn from the true masters.

From the very the first day, my Pilates instructor, Hanna, told me that there was nothing wrong with my knees. She explained that the discomfort in my knees was due to a postural misalignment, caused by my chronic lower back injury. She told me that I would not need an operation, and that I would eventually recover from my back injury if I followed a proper exercise regime. She reassured me that I would soon be free of pain and enjoying a stronger, healthier body.

From that moment, I was hooked. I attended my Pilates exercise programme regularly, three times a week. The pain slowly faded, and I became, day-by-day, healthier and stronger.

I was so fascinated by the approach of this intelligent exercise method that I decided to make a career out of it. I felt the need to share this intriguing new approach of exercise with others who, like me, needed to know about it.

I had a new mission!

How many people were out there in the world, like me, in pain, frustrated, hopeless, not knowing what to do, or doing all the wrong things, the wrong exercises, seeing the wrong professionals? How many had been told that "going under the knife" was their only option? **These people needed to know**, to be told, to be educated. They had a right to know!

At that point, I made a huge U-turn in my career. I had been studying at the prestigious Laban Centre in London to become a choreographer, and a dance and movement expert.

Now I wanted to focus my studies on Intelligent Movement. I had decided to become a Movement Therapist.

MY HEALING AND THE CHANGE IN ME: NO MORE PAIN, AND FINALLY THE GAIN

After I started healing my body with the help of the Pilates Method, I noticed that my back pain had disappeared, my knees had stopped bothering me and, best of all, to my great surprise my body was not only getting stronger by the day, but it was also changing shape quite noticeably. I was becoming fitter and more toned. People asked me what I was doing to look so good, to be in such great shape. Whatever secret I had they wanted me to share it with them; they wanted to do the same thing I was doing. Everyone who saw me said, "If I can look like you, by doing what you do, you've got me!"

The truth is that I was no longer exercising like crazy the way I did during my dancing years, doing exhausting hours of training every day. I was not sweating it out at the gym like most of my friends; I was not getting up at 6 am for a daily jog as some other friends were doing and feeling exhausted for the rest of the day. I was moving in a natural, comfortable and very efficient way, yet my results were far more striking. My body looked younger, defined and more toned; I felt rejuvenated. I felt full of energy.

What I had come to understand was that life was not about driving myself to exhaustion to be fit and to look good. I no longer had to live by the maxim "No pain, no gain!"; it was not about the number of hours spent exercising and sweating. It was about **quality.** For me, it was about finding the right movement connection and the **right equation, in which the results matched my effort.** It was about finding a way to move that most suited my body, and my movement personality.

I am an ex-dancer and a very active person. At the same time, I have a history of back injury. I personally needed to challenge my body's performance, while at the same time I had to take appropriate precautions. My back injury would reappear at any time should I choose an inappropriate exercise programme.

I knew that whether I spent two or three hours a week or one hour a day exercising in an intelligent way, the results had to match my effort.

After so many years of doing the wrong things, I had finally understood, my body was healed, and I simply felt great!

Ten years after my original back injury, I was living in Singapore, enjoying a totally pain-free life and, as a bonus, a very strong and youthful body. I was in my late 40s but looked and felt younger than ever.

My transformation had been a long journey. Yes, 10 years is a long time, but the wait had been worth it.

The Pilates Method had helped me enormously; my studies in post-rehabilitation and intelligent movement methods had given me an even deeper understanding of the body and the tools with which to help others.

But, finally, what truly made the difference was the chance I had to work with my clients, of listening over and over again to the different stories of people who, like me, had suffered a chronic pain condition, who, like me, had tried everything with no results. It was while observing their bodies and their movement patterns that I finally created my BODY ID Method.

These people, my wonderful clients, were my inspiration and my true teachers.

By sharing their stories, listening to them and observing their bodies and their movement patterns I started to understand more and more about the nature of their injuries and how to improve their lifestyle... and, as a bonus, their appearance.

I understood that if they followed an intelligent exercise regime that was perfectly designed to their specific body and personal needs, their BODY ID, they would recover and, like me, enjoy a life free of pain and regain a more youthful appearance.

Maintaining the body in the correct movement and alignment was the key. But the right key was to choose for these people the most **appropriate movement and exercise programme for them, individually**.

I had religiously applied those principles to my own body, and this was the time of my true transformation. I was now in my 50s but, certainly, my body and my spirit felt much younger.

I lived in, and ran, my own very successful business in Singapore, the very first Pilates and Movement Therapy Centre in all southeast Asia (it was 1998).

I was finally in control of my body and in control of my life. I felt strong and confident, but, most important of all, I knew the pain would never come back. I had rediscovered the joy of movement, the elation of going for a long walk, being able to carry my groceries and my suitcases when I travelled, and the ability to go back to my passion, dancing, with the freedom and the joy that I had forgotten.

You may think 10 years to get rid of my pain was a long time. I agree! It might have taken me a long time, a lifetime of practice, study and understanding, but I can assure you it will take you only **a few months** if you accept my guidance and follow my advice, step by step.

Over the years, I have applied my method to my clients with the most amazing results. I have understood how to make that difference.

There are a number of true stories and client cases in this book. They all have a very happy ending, just like my story. Hopefully, there will be one to which you can relate.

You may ask, what do I do that is so different in order to succeed so successfully in the full recovery of my patients?

In order to understand their body and the nature of the injury and help them during the process of their recovery, I apply my comprehensive approach, taking into consideration many different aspects, such as their lifestyle, body type, clinical history and personality. I strongly believe that it is not the person who has to adapt her/his body to a particular exercise routine; on the contrary, each chosen movement needs to be adapted to the person's specific needs. A truly bespoke exercise programme that has only your name on it.

CHAPTER 2

THE RIGHT
Equation

How many of us have spent several months, or a few years, or maybe even a lifetime trying to get rid of a persistent backache, trying to get fitter, trying to craft a new body, or simply trying to improve our posture? How much time, sweat and effort have we invested with NO VISIBLE RESULTS, WRONG RESULTS, or in fact, no satisfaction whatsoever... or JUST A FEELING OF FRUSTRATION? Or, even worse, and a very common scenario, how many of us have energetically entered into a programme only to end up injured; with pulled or torn muscles, with serious back problems, or damaged knees, and have consequently been forced to give up our favourite sport or activity because we were advised to do so by a health professional?

We were simply not applying **the right equation. Our efforts did not equal the expected results.**

THE MYTH OF EXERCISE

Some of the most common injuries I see in my practice are caused by the wrong choice, or improper practice of exercise programmes. It is becoming a very worrying phenomenon indeed.

This means that the information that is out there is not sufficient and often incorrect. We go by the latest fad we read about in magazines, or by the friend who swears by a gym or by a particular exercise or sport that changed his/her life or taken by an impulse, one day we decide that we want to get fitter and lose a few extra pounds, so we join the gym next to our office without professional guidance and body awareness.

During my career I have been featured in many newspapers and magazines but believe me, I have rejected an equal number of interviews and articles simply because those magazines were only interested in giving the public superficial and often not useful information. They only wanted to write about how to get a lifted and firmer butt or a flat tummy and had no interest in educating the public in making more conscious and intelligent choices.

I understand that this kind of easy information can sell much better, but I strongly believe that someone has to take on the responsibility to inform the public in a correct way. This has been my mission over the past 20 years.

The truth is that out there is a jungle of information or, rather, misinformation.

FAST-FOOD EXERCISE

The result is that we live in a world today of "fast-food exercise", that burger recipe that is cooked in the same way in thousands of fast-food kitchens around the world. It is inexpensive and fast, but in order to maintain a low cost/high sale ratio, the quality gets totally lost.

The old idea of physical exercise and physical education has today radically changed, sadly, and not always in a positive way. In a world of mass information, there is no filter, the so-called "word of mouth" is disappearing. You just need to have a look at the web today where you are bombarded with applications and photos showing you how to get fitter; how to get a better body in a few weeks, or a sexy chocolate-bar-shaped six-pack. I look at these applications with horror and recognize that most of them could be very harmful to the public.

Imagine now a different scenario.

Instead of suffering from a backache you suffer, for example, from a digestive problem. You go to see a nutritional specialist. You will go through a very detailed protocol where the specialist will ask you many questions concerning your lifestyle, eating habits, current diet, and medical history, and most of the time very specific allergy tests are required. All this information is absolutely necessary to create a safe dietary regime.

Those same principles should be applied when choosing an exercise programme.

In order to understand a person's body and, in the case of an injury, to help the person during the process of his/her recovery, I apply my comprehensive approach, taking into consideration many different aspects of the person's life, lifestyle, posture, movement history, and clinical history.

It is not the person's body that has to adapt to a particular exercise method; on the contrary, the movement and exercise programme needs to adapt to the person's specific needs and lifestyle; a truly bespoke movement and exercise programme created for your unique BODY ID.

- *So often we have not chosen an appropriate programme for our particular Body Type simply because we did not know any better.*

- *We have never given any consideration to what kind of exercise or sport is most suited for us, and our lifestyle.*

- *We have not sought the right professional advice for a persistent ache or a chronic pain, and most likely we did not choose the right place or the right instructor to guide us through this important process of healing and transformation.*

All the above are the necessary ingredients to create your ideal exercise regime in order to, finally, achieve the expected results. By applying my principles when choosing a movement and exercise programme, specially created for your BODY ID, you will finally achieve what I call **the right equation**:

$$\text{"EFFORT} = \text{RESULT"}$$

Remember, some of the most important elements of our intelligent choices are to recognize that:

Our body is unique and different from anyone else's. An exercise programme that is good for Mr A might not be suitable, or even damaging, for Mrs B.

The exercise programme has to adapt to our body, and not our body to the exercise programme.

The qualifications and the experience of the instructor have to be fully trusted, and trustworthy.

Our exercise programme needs to fit us the same way a perfectly tailored dress/suit would fit us. We need to choose a custom-made programme suitable for our personal needs. I always give my clients the same metaphor.

TAILOR-MADE

Imagine that one day you decide to have a dress/suit made for a very important occasion. You want to look your best, and you want to feel different and very special. You are not going to pick an off-the-rack dress/suit from a department store. You must have something personalized. More YOU, totally UNIQUE to enhance your body shape, and created for your personal need.

So, you go to an experienced, reputable tailor.

You discuss the occasion for which you need your outfit.

You choose a style that best suits **you** and your **body shape**. You discuss the fabrics, the colours and design that would best suit your **personalit**y and your personal style and taste and, most importantly, **you get measured.**

You go for a few fittings, and VOILA! Your dream dress or immaculate suit is ready for you. When you finally wear it, it feels so comfortable, so perfectly... unique. It simply FITS YOU like a glove, just as you imagined it would.

This is the way you should choose your exercise programme, custom-made, specially designed for you, fitted to enhance your body shape, and adapted to your movement personality and personal needs.

EXERCISE HAUTE COUTURE

The secret for tailoring an exercise programme to the person's specific needs is to develop an eye for detail, to become, first of all, an intelligent observer. A good instructor, like a good tailor, needs to observe and understand your posture alignment and your movement patterns. These movement patterns are not always the correct ones. The body is a very intelligent vehicle; it adapts to different environments and situations. Our muscles will adapt to an injury, to a postural misalignment, or to a sedentary lifestyle.

If you practise exercise routines incorrectly in a body that is posturally misaligned, you will do more damage than good. Those incorrect movement patterns and the subsequent muscle compensations can easily become the root of chronic pain or an injury.

UNDERSTANDING THE STORY OF YOUR BODY

It is a fact that as we grow older our body starts a process of natural degeneration. But we can see this from a different and more positive perspective:

As we grow wiser our body has a story to tell. It is written in every inch of our body, in our muscles, in our posture, in our movements, in our shape. I have simply learned to read these signs, and, with my help, I would like you to learn to read them too. I will teach you to develop that body and movement awareness that will help you to improve your health, the quality of your lifestyle and, finally, your appearance.

I have observed during the years I have been teaching that, with the application of the right equation, changes happen very quickly. In a few weeks, people tell me that the pain has gone; in a few months they can not only feel the difference in their body but also see it.

They all enjoy a different lifestyle, in which they can move freely, pain-free, and are able to go back to their favourite sport or activity if they want to. They even enjoy a new, fit and healthy figure. And, of course, with all this comes a wonderful sensation, **confidence,** and the elation of feeling good and looking good. This is what I call a true transformation.

I have planned this book as a manual. There will be many opportunities for you not just to read about what you can do, but also to practise simple activities to achieve what you want.

I would like to pause now and practise our first visualization exercise. This will help you to have a better and clearer understanding of your BODY ID.

EXERCISE
Visualization

Visualization is a very powerful tool in intelligent movement; after all, it all starts in your mind.

To do this visualization exercise I would like you to sit somewhere comfortably, relax, close your eyes, and take some time to go through your life from the time you were a child until today.

Go back to when you were a child. See yourself happy, bouncing, running and jumping with the freedom of a young body and spirit. Your body had no limitations. Go through the changes of your adolescence; recognize what these changes have brought to your body shape and to your personality.

Then go through your life as an adult until today and see the different stages of your body growth and the changes that have occurred. How has your body changed and adapted during these natural life cycles?

Think about your time as a student, your marriage, your children, your job; what changes can you identify?

Ask yourself, is your lifestyle quite sedentary?

Have you had an accident or an illness that has caused you pain or discomfort?

Have you experienced a sad event that has caused you sorrow?

All this will be written in your body.

This is the story of your body.

Think now about your mother and father and your siblings.

Do you see yourself in them? Do you recognize the similarities in your and their body shapes? I want you to do this because it is hard to recognize oddities in your own body and much easier to observe them in someone else. Most structural body imbalances such as scoliosis, flat feet, knock knees or a curved or hunched back are hereditary.

Close your eyes... take your time... see yourself through these phases of your life, and most of all be kind to yourself.

If you like, you can also take some written notes; you can create your own BODY wish board – it's fun! Go through your pictures of yourself from when you were a child to your most recent ones. You can see now how your body has changed throughout the different stages of your life. Accept these changes with love. They are part of your life, of your own story.

Only when you can recognize and accept these changes will you be able to make the transformation.

Now focus on the area of your body you would like to improve, to change, or where you are in pain. See already those changes happening as part of your new body. Set your target and believe in it. Remember that you will are the only person who can really make that change.

JADE'S STORY

Jade's story is a perfect example of the application of the right equation.

Like most of my clients, Jade came to see me as a last resort. A mutual friend had suggested that she see me. She thought, she said, "since I had tried everything else, one more try can't hurt." As Jade told me later, she did not want to disappoint our mutual friend who had so kindly given to her as a present a Postural Assessment with me.

After years of trying all kinds of exercises, including yoga, gym, personal training, the latest exercise trends, even Pilates, Jade had reached a point of total frustration. Nothing worked. There were no changes, no transformations, just sweat and fatigue accompanied by the frustration of spending so much **effort, time, energy and money** on activities **that did not give her any results.**

Despite practising all these different exercise methods, Jade's body had gained quite a few pounds over the past few years, especially around the middle part of the body.

Jade had an Athletic build. She belonged to the Athletic body type (see Chapter 5, Body Types)

She was not happy about her figure. She felt heavy and hated, as she told me during our first meeting, her big tummy. Her strong build was now showing a bit too much bulk. Her clothes did not fit properly. She felt uncomfortable and, as the French say so well, she did not feel "well in her skin".

But most of all, Jade was experiencing increasing frustration. Why, she wanted to know, after all these years of effort, had nothing positive happened? In fact, her body had not only not improved but seemed to be deteriorating.

Physically

Her posture had suffered because of the weight increase, and consequentially, Jade suffered from back and knee pain. Exercising was becoming more difficult and more uncomfortable.

Emotionally

Jade was frustrated, because the more effort she put in, the fewer were the results she got back. She was fed up. She found relief from her frustration in food. She would swing from extreme diets to comfort eating.

Practically

She had invested time and money in something that did not pay off.

After a long chat and a detailed Postural Assessment her case was very clear to me.

She had applied the wrong equation.

Her Efforts did not equal Results (E ≠ R).

It was not Jade's fault.

During all these years Jade had not been properly guided or advised.

First of all, Jade needed to reconnect with her own body. In order to make the transformation she had dreamed of for so many years, she needed to understand and accept who she was.

She had to make peace with herself and her body.

Her Athletic body type needed a suitable exercise regime and she needed to understand the guidelines for her BODY TYPE.

She needed the right food for her muscles.

Her body type, The Athletic/Pitta, bulks very easily; too much high-impact exercise or any gym weight programme is not suitable for a woman who wants to maintain a slender and more feminine shape – and she had done far too much of that.

The gym programme she had followed had not been suitable for her particular case. The personal trainers were pushing her in the wrong direction, putting her back at risk, bulking her muscles, and making her feel exhausted.

Following a friend's advice, Jade had joined **yoga** classes. Her back pain had worsened, and her neck and shoulders were very tight. She was attending very large group classes, and she could not get the appropriate attention.

Pilates was the suggestion of another friend. But Jade ended up in the wrong hands, with a non-qualified instructor and an unsuitable programme. She was very disappointed with the Pilates experience, and achieved no results.

After trying all of the above methods an even more frustrated Jade went into exercise frenzy, trying every possible new **exercise trend.** The more she tried, the less she achieved, and the worse she felt.

Having had no positive results from exercising and with the determination to lose some extra pounds, Jade then went for detox programmes, special retreats and different diets.

The only things she ended up losing were time, money and trust.

By the time I met Jade a couple of years ago, she was again exercising with a personal trainer who was teaching her the most unsuitable exercises for her body type and personal needs. Another disaster!

After telling me her frustrating exercise history, Jade broke down in tears, sobbing and telling me that she could not take it anymore. She was tired, fed up and broke.

Sad to say, I have heard this story many times over the years of my career as a Movement Therapist.

Jade needed to apply the Right Equation.

She needed the right professional to guide her into this process of transformation.

Jade needed a programme specifically designed for her personal needs.

The exercise programme had to suit:

- Her Body Type

Athletic body type (see Chapter 5, BODY TYPES)

- Her Life Style

Jade worked for a renowned PR company, and her appearance was very important to her.

- Her Personality

Jade had no problem with being disciplined about exercising, but she had become more and more obsessed with her body. She focused too much on the negative aspect of it, and she felt inadequate. This feeling of inadequacy eventually even caused her to avoid personal relationships and to find comfort in food. She was caught in a vicious circle.

How could I help Jade?

1.   **Educate** her about a healthier lifestyle.

2.   **Guide** her with love and care and give her back the trust she had lost in herself and her body.

3.   **Help** her to reconnect the Mind and Body and help to find that lost connection.

4.   **Create** a suitable exercise regime for her Body Type and Movement personality.

This is the approach that a good professional in any movement or exercise method should have taken with Jade but, unfortunately, it had not happened. That is why she did not get any results.

Needless to say Jade's story, like all of my stories, has a very happy ending.

Once again it was hard to convince Jade, after so many years of trying too hard, that the **No Pain, Yes Gain** route was the right direction to take.

I designed a very personalized programme for Jade, first of all to develop a better postural awareness and then to realign her body.

Eventually Jade went back to the gym, where I advised an appropriate light cardio exercise regime, and enjoyed very much her weekly yoga. I guided her on how to choose a qualified Pilates instructor and enjoy the results of this intelligent method.

As she started to reconnect to her body Jade switched to a much healthier diet, as she no longer felt that impulse to find comfort in food.

But for Jade it was not only the exercises that made the difference, but also how I guided her to reconnect with her body. She finally accepted who she was, she discovered her strengths, she was in control of her body. She had learned about her BODY ID, her body type, her movement personality, and by applying the guidelines I had suggested she was finally able to transform her weaknesses into strengths.

Most of all she was no longer focusing on the negative aspect of her body, she was now relaxed and accepting. She enjoyed and participated in her journey in movement with great enthusiasm.

Jade was finally happy; her movements were now flowing effortlessly, and changes were finally happening.

This time she had applied the right equation:

RIGHT EFFORT = RESULT

And the transformation had finally happened.

With the application of my principles Jade thrived.

She became her body's best friend.

She learned to listen to her body, to nurture it, to understand it and, finally, to challenge it in the right way.

The results were amazing.

A gorgeous, shapely butterfly broke out of her cocoon in just a few months, ready to spread her beautiful wings and fly.

The bulk had gone; the extra pounds had effortlessly disappeared. A beautiful, confident and happy Jade was now attending her PR functions feeling and looking like a million dollars! People were now looking at her svelte and confident posture body and complimenting her.

QUESTIONNAIRE

The questionnaire below will be very useful to achieve a better understanding of your Body Type and Movement personality. It will also help you to do your own evaluation and choose the best exercise programme for your personal needs.

Take a pen and paper and:

1. List the exercise programmes, or sports programmes you have followed since you were a child.

SPORTS

Past ....

....

....

....

....

Current ....

....

....

....

....

GYM

Past ....

....

....

....

....

Current ....

....

....

....

....

OTHER ACTIVITIES

Past ....

....

....

....

....

Current ....

....

....

....

....

2. If you have stopped any exercise programme, list your reasons for doing so.

- ☐ Too busy at work/with family
- ☐ Medical
- ☐ An injury, an illness, or pain
- ☐ Personal (for example: too busy, in a relationship, work, children)
- ☐ No results with past exercise regimes
- ☐ Tired of trying
- ☐ Laziness

3. If you are currently following one or more exercise programmes, make a list of the benefits you are getting from it.

- ☐ Fitter
- ☐ More toned
- ☐ Weight loss
- ☐ Stronger
- ☐ More stamina
- ☐ Help in the rehabilitation of an injury
- ☐ Better posture
- ☐ Improved performance in sports
- ☐ Feel better
- ☐ Others...

*4. If you are **not following** a specific exercise programme, list what you would like to do, and what you would expect from it.*

WHAT ACTIVITIES/SPORTS I WOULD LIKE TO DO

....

....

....

....

....

....

....

....

....

....

....

MY GOALS

....

....

....

....

....

....

....

....

....

....

FROM CAVE TO CUBICLE

From Homo Sapiens to "Homo Computeriensis"

Cave people did not have to worry about fitness or how to keep their body in movement. For our ancestors, it was all about survival. Their body had to perform at its best; they had to be alert and aware of the surrounding danger 24/7. Our brave ancestors had to be strong and always ready to face the ultimate challenges of daily life.

I believe very few of us in our modern lifestyle would relate well to such a harsh reality.

This dependence on the body for survival has continued for millennia, through civilization after civilization. Men used to hunt, walk, run, climb, ride and fight. Women gave birth, worked in the fields from dawn until sunset, carried the water from the well to the home, washed the clothes in the river, and carried their children on their backs during the long, harsh working days.

Honestly, I can't think of a harder gym workout. I believe that the typical daily bodily effort of our ancestors would not even compare with the most challenging work out of a contemporary competitive athlete.

Today we face the challenges but also the advantages of a Contemporary Body.

So, as we understand it, our lifestyle has dramatically changed, and thankfully improved in many aspects. Life expectancy has increased, but our body's performance has sadly decreased.

Let's think about this for a moment. We have spent all this time "in movement", then suddenly, within a comparatively short number of years, with the advent of the "Industrial Revolution" our life in movement has stopped. I strongly believe that humankind has not yet adapted to it. The changes in our lifestyle have been too sudden. We are facing a more sedentary and less movement-orientated lifestyle and we are already paying the price.

From *Homo Sapiens* we turned into a new species, *Homo Computeriensis*.

Today we live and enjoy the convenience of a more comfortable modern lifestyle. Who needs to walk, run, climb or ride? We have many different modes of transport now. Instead of toiling in the fields and hunting for food we have sedentary jobs, often sitting at a desk in front of a computer.

We have the convenience of the supermarkets and the many labour-saving devices in our homes that allow us more time for inactive leisure such as television, smartphones and computers. We shop online and live in a sedentary virtual world.

Of course, we are blessed to have more leisure time than our ancestors, whose life was all about survival, but this inactivity and the way we have adapted to it is the source of the problems, the chronic aches and pains, weight issues, and related illnesses that plague our contemporary society.

The sad truth is that, at the end of our daily tasks, no matter if we have been doing a lot of brain gym at the desk, in front of the PC, in a boardroom, or have achieved an amazing deal, have gained the best yearly bonus, have run around the house, the kitchen, and the children, we have forgotten and neglected our most precious tool: OUR BODY.

Which is there, craving to be used, to be moved, to be challenged, to be listened to, and to be nurtured. In our modern lifestyle we are so busy with our life, career, marriage, children, etc., we feel that we have lost a part of ourselves, our body. We look sadly in the mirror and we don't recognize ourselves. We complain about being unfit. We complain of our aches and pains.

Remember, it is **never too late.**

It is time to rediscover that lost connection, that Body Intelligence that has enabled us to survive on this earth for hundreds and thousands of years. This is the same body intelligence that allows a small child to take the first steps of life, to run and tumble, and to climb trees with impunity. This same connection has enabled some of my clients and friends (see their stories in Chapter 11, The Healing Power of Movement) to defeat the impediments of life-threatening illnesses. It is also that connection that has dramatically improved the quality of many other people's lives. Lastly, this same connection has helped me to maintain a healthy and youthful body into my 60s.

THE DIFFERENCE BETWEEN MALE AND FEMALE BODIES

Let's go back to the origins

The differences between male and female sexes are anatomical and physiological.

I have always been a big supporter of male and female equality. We are very blessed to live in a time where this is reflected in our society more than ever before. But we still have to accept that male and female bodies are physiologically and anatomically different.

As in the animal world, the differentiation between male and female is all based on the role each sex has within the law of reproduction, and so it has been since cave-dwelling times. The female carried the children, gave birth, cared for them and looked after the cave, making sure the shelter was cosy and warm, prepared the food and the safety of her children. The male hunted, provided food and fought for the protection of his cave family.

Today in our modern "cubicle" world there is no longer such differentiation of roles. Male and female hunt equally on the same grounds. This is wonderful! I am blessed to be living in this era of equality. I always make a joke that if I had lived a few hundred years ago my forward thinking would have certainly taken me to the stake.

So, going back to our different physiology, YES, we are different, and we need to accept and understand it. This is not a question of who is stronger or weaker, or who has the better intellectual capacity, but truly of how the female and the male body operate differently due to the necessities of reproduction.

THE FEMALE BODY

The child-bearer

The female body is dominated by female hormones, such as oestrogen and progesterone. These hormones lead our development during the different phases of a woman's life; also, they make the miracle of life happen, childbirth! A woman's well-being depends on that perfectly fine-tuned hormonal balance.

We were raised to believe that the female body was created to conceive, give birth, reproduce, and to provide a safe environment for her progeny.

I know that some of you ladies might grin at this idea, or might not agree with me at this point, but please consider my explanation simply from a scientific point of view. The survival of the species is the ultimate purpose of our existence.

The pelvic power

Our pelvis is the centre of our femininity as it holds our reproductive organs. It is powerful! But unfortunately, as powerful as it might be, we lose our pelvic power as a consequence of pregnancies, menopause and hormonal fluctuations.

Advised exercises for a female body.

When it comes to exercise, sadly, I have not seen trainers taking our female constitution much into consideration. Most of the programmes I see in gyms are unfortunately designed mainly for a male body, and we women have to adapt and even prove we can be as strong to prove our equality. Unless you are an athlete or an elite mover, extreme and exhausting training programmes do not work for the female body simply because our body has not been designed to be challenged like a hunter or a fighter.

So, what happens when the female body is pushed too hard? It goes into adrenal stress and this creates havoc in that incredibly engineered but yet delicate hormonal balance; it's just like throwing an orchestra out of tune.

We are strong in a very enduring way, and we should not compare our physiological strength with the male...

Over the years, I have witnessed so many women being pushed into most unsuitable exercise programmes. Many suffered bad injuries, others were exhausted and fatigued as they had to juggle family, children and demanding careers as well as exhausting physical programmes, and others could not even conceive as their body was put under so much stress.

The results, along with stress, exhaustion and hormonal imbalance, are many:

- *Undesired body shape*

- *Too much muscle, resulting in no longer fitting into their clothes*

- *Weight gain*

- *A less feminine look*

- *Muscle's tension, aches and pains*

- *Chronic injuries*

Why? Simply because these gym or exercise programmes were designed for MEN.

So, which are the best exercise programmes for women? Before I advise you, I would like to begin by looking at the different phases of a woman's life, from puberty to mature age:

- *Puberty*

- *Pre-natal 20s to 30s*

- *Post-natal 30s to 40s*

- *Pre-menopause 40s to 50s*

- *Menopause 50s*

- *Post-menopause 60s on*

SUGGESTED PROGRAMMES FOR THE FEMALE BODY

It's quite simple; we can do any exercise or any sport as long as we understand our BODY ID, and we avoid interfering with our hormonal balance.

I always suggest having a very balanced exercise programme, just as you would plan a healthy and well-calibrated meal. For example, some cardio, some resistance training, some outdoor activity such as walking, and some stretching. You can also combine a favourite sport, dance, yoga, Pilates and many more (see Chapter 12, INTELLIGENT MOVEMENT, INTELLIGENT CHOICES).

Some women prefer high-impact exercise, some prefer low-impact. Some go for the quiet yoga studio, some for a more intimate Pilates' studio, while others will prefer the gym or outdoor activities. It's all good for you if you choose according to your BODY ID, meaning your **movement personality and body type**. Never force your body to do an activity that does not resonate with you just because someone is telling you to do so, whether they be a friend or a trainer or someone you have just seen online.

My suggestions are simple to follow:

- *Understand first of all your BODY ID by following my guidelines in Chapter 5, Body Types.*

- *Find the style of exercise that most suits you.*

- *Understand your movement personality and which environment suits you best.*

- *Keep a variety of movement programmes, just as in a healthy meal you would include different ingredients.*

- *Never compromise on quality of instruction.*

FEMALE BODY CHARACTERISTICS

- *Softer, curvier*
- *The fat distribution of the female body will depend on the body type (see Chapter 5, BODY TYPES)*
- *The Slim VATA*
- *The Athletic PITTA*
- *The Voluptuous KAPHA*

Female Strength, Pelvic Power: Well, what more can I say? We carry life and give birth.

Weaknesses: Most probably our hormonal fluctuations.

WOMEN'S HORMONAL PHASES AND THEIR DECADES

Puberty

This is when our body prepares to celebrate our femininity, and we start menstruating.

Suggested exercise

This is the age when many young girls start learning a sport, join a school team, or a dance school. It is a very important time and age to lay the foundations for healthy movement patterns and good posture. The body is so malleable, and it learns quickly.

Our contemporary body challenges

- *School – poor sitting environment, leading to bad postural habits.*

- *Tablets and smartphones, leading to a more sedentary lifestyle.*

- *Schools – poor physical education programmes.*

- *Social media – body image issues.*

The 20s

During our 20s we feel at the peak of life, our body has great muscle tone, our skin is smooth, our metabolism works at its best and we can afford that post-party late night pizza without the devastating effects of the day-after guilt. And it's all about falling in love! We want to look beautiful, and Nature wants us to find a mate.

Suggested exercise

Anything is good if we follow my body type guidelines and if we maintain healthy habits such as a healthy diet, and good postural and movement awareness. Practising a favourite sport is good for the body and for the mind.

Our contemporary body challenges

- *Too much time sitting in front of a computer, tablet, smartphones.*

- *Unsuitable exercise programmes.*

- *Unsafe online classes.*

- *Lack of safe exercise guidelines.*

- *Social media body image issues.*

The 30s

In our contemporary age, in our 30s is the time when most women have children. It is essential that women follow specific pre- and post- pregnancy protocols and safe pre- and post- natal exercise programmes (see Chapter 10, WOMEN'S HEALTH). This will avoid many potential future complications.

Our contemporary body challenges

The ONE and MOST important challenge:

- *Women not following the necessary pre- and post- natal protocols and exercise programmes recommended by qualified specialists.*

It's a recipe for disaster...

The 40s

Women in their 40s are often divided into 2 categories:

- *The ones who seem to have forgotten their body.*
- *The ones who decide to restore their body after years of family, children or career responsibilities.*

These, of course, do not include elite movers and sports professionals who, like me, had to continue their physical training despite family obligations.

Our contemporary body challenges

- *Lack of proper guidance and information.*
- *Exercise programmes devised by unqualified trainers.*
- *Unsuitable programmes and environments.*
- *Chronic pain and injuries.*
- *Lack of results despite best efforts (see Chapter 2, THE RIGHT EQUATION)*

From the 50s on...

The Silver age and the Golden rule

This is the time of harvesting, the time of truth.

What we did or did not do looking after our body during the previous decades will manifest now...

THE GOLDEN RULE:

Never Stop Moving

Our contemporary body challenges

- *Women are most challenged by menopause and hormonal changes.*

- *Our body goes through some unwanted but natural body changes.*

- *Osteoporosis.*

- *Urinary incontinence.*

- *Painful intercourse.*

- *Slower metabolism.*

- *As our weight goes up our confidence goes down.*

- *We do not recognise the woman trapped in that body…*

- *Panic! Mood swings, mental fog*

- *We do not feel sexy.*

- *We think: I give up because I am old.*

We can't give up, EVER – a woman can be stunning and feel sexy way after her 50s; it is our right.

SOLUTIONS

- *Maintain a healthy hormonal balance.*

- *Keep moving and practising safe exercise programmes.*

- *Maintain a healthy diet, and healthy habits.*

- *Keep a positive attitude and move on with the times, live the present and do not stay stuck in the past. IT'S THE NOW that counts.*

- *Learn new things and new skills every day.*

- *Spend time with young people, they have a lot to teach us.*
- *Celebrate your ageless body and mind.*

If you stop, you become OLD!

THE MALE BODY

The hunter, the fighter

"Me Tarzan, you Jane."

This phrase comes to my mind from my childhood, my memory of the movie *Tarzan*. Our ultimate handsome, wild, sexy and muscled hero fought the jungle elements to protect his beautiful and delicate Jane. What did Jane have to do? Just be beautiful and take care of the little treehouse they lived in with lovely Cheeta, the chimpanzee.

Yes, sadly those were the kind of stories we baby boomers were given during the 50s and 60s. Fortunately, they were the last of those unrealistic preconceptions... The 70s and feminism were just around the corner... today, women can be soldiers, astronauts, Formula 1 champions, you name it, anything we want, with no physical or intellectual limitations.

So, what happened to our Tarzan?

For thousands of years, men hunted, conquered, fought wars, defended their homes. Yes, men could carry heavy weapons and other objects, build great monuments; they had to be strong, VERY STRONG.

The male body was prepared from puberty to be challenged by dangerous and enduring physical challenges; it was the law of "the strongest will survive". From his youth to the end of his life a man had to be constantly manly: hunt, fight, conquer, defend and protect and, eventually, die with courage and dignity.

The male body is dominated by the testosterone hormone. This hormone plays a key role in male sexual development, it stimulates sperm production and the male sex drive. Testosterone also affects male body characteristics, such as increased muscle, bone mass and body hair. All this was needed over the millennia as the male had to be strong to conquer, reproduce, and provide protection for his progeny.

In our contemporary society, Tarzan has fallen from the trees into an office chair, and he is stuck at his desk in front of a screen. He fights the wars of the modern world, hunts for money, conquers for better career positions, and defends his financial possessions. His main tool today is his brain; the better educated he is, the more career opportunities there are for him… and, of course, the ultimate goal is: MORE MONEY, MORE POWER.

His strong body and muscles are no longer needed for survival in this modern world. Machines, weapons and technology are replacing his physical power. Mental endurance has replaced physical endurance.

Women, too, are out there hunting in the same grounds, using the same weapons, searching like men for the same ultimate goals: SUCCESS, POWER and MONEY. Equal soldiers and fighters in this contemporary search for survival.

Men's contemporary body challenges

The dramatic change of lifestyle is leading men to:

- *Office work – a sedentary lifestyle*

- *Loss of muscle mass*

- *A higher likelihood of injuries when exercising or practising sport*

- *Chronic pain*

- *Weight gain and related illnesses*

- *Lack of time for physical activities*

- *A drop in testosterone*

How to solve it?

Most of my clients in my practice in London are men. They are my superheroes and range from their 20s to their 80s. Athletes, businessmen, doctors, men recovering from injuries, illnesses, or simply men who decided to have a deeper and more intelligent approach towards exercising.

Why do they come to me? Because they are searching for a different approach and solution for their bodies. These are the issues I hear the most:

- *I am in pain because I have been hurt by the wrong exercise programme.*

- *My doctor told me I have to exercise to get better, but as soon as I move, I am in more pain; I feel so frustrated!*

- *I am sitting all day at the office and my back is killing me.*

- *I am stuck, I am putting on weight and I have no energy.*

- *I am in constant pain; I have tried everything; you are my last chance.*

- *My doctor prescribed your posture and movement education programme; what do you do, exactly?*

- *I miss playing my favourite sport; I don't dare to do it because, every time I try, I spend the next few days in pain.*

I hear these stories every day in my practice.

My approach with the male body is different from the one I use with women. I have to think and communicate differently, more like an engineer who is dealing with the owner and driver of a beautiful Ferrari car. I need to identify first the source of the mechanical fault. Then the plan is how to fix it to achieve the ultimate goal of "High Performance".

New and correct movement patterns need to be installed in the muscle memory, and, just like a powerful Ferrari, the correct mechanical alignment, along with a strong engine, driven by a very skilled driver, our brain, will maximize the performance of the vehicle. To maintain a healthy and steady body performance I will finally create a new and healthier exercise programme.

My success rate is very high! And most of my Super Guys are now enjoying a healthy and balanced sport and movement programme free from aches and pain.

HOW TO RECONNECT
With Our Body

L ife is not static. From the very first spark that was the creation of our universe (the Big Bang), from that first instant, there has been an ever-expanding moving force. We may call this "Energy", or "God's Will", but one thing is for sure, **Life is Movement.**

We witness this every day of our life. This ever-expanding moving force has created galaxies, stars, our solar system and life on earth... there would not be life without movement.

So it is for humans and our physical body. From the moment of conception, we begin to grow and move following the natural pattern of eternal growth and the eternal movement of the universe.

Nothing is static in our lives. Everything is moving, growing and dying, following the natural pattern of the circle of life.

Sometimes we forget that our body has been given to us to move. It is our perfect vehicle, a perfectly engineered one, a small universe on wheels, which needs to be nurtured, understood and ultimately driven with the skill and the passion of a Formula 1 driver. This perfect vehicle is meant to be kept in motion, maintained, fine-tuned, loved, and not discarded and forgotten like an old bicycle in our basement, where it will rust and deteriorate. And just like the old bike, when we dust it off to go for a ride, our body, if it is no longer in good repair, will eventually break down, leaving us in despair in the middle of our life journey.

OUR BODY NEEDS TO BE KEPT IN MOVEMENT.

Lack of movement creates static energy, and static energy creates blockages at different levels:

1.   *On a physical level, blockages will create pain and illnesses.*

2. *On a mental level, blockages will create disturbances of the mind and body.*

If our body is the perfect vehicle for our souls, or more pragmatically put, if our body is the vehicle we are driving through this life, we had better take great care of it.

Imagine if our body were the ultimate sports car; a Ferrari or Lamborghini that we have always dreamed of owning since we were a child. After working so hard to get it, believe me, we would really take good care of it. It would never be neglected. We would drive it every day with pride and pleasure. We would have it serviced regularly by an expert mechanic. We would polish it. We would take it for a run regularly to make sure that its engine kept roaring at its maximum potential. What a treasure! And what a pleasure to drive! So why would we care for our body with less diligence?

The truth is that we take our body for granted. This magnificent vehicle we are born with is used and very often abused, and eventually left to rust in the basement of our busy, frantic lives.

What can we do? How can we take care of our body? How do we make the right choices? Do we really understand what we need to do, to keep the vehicle running, our body moving?

In a world where an overdose of conflicting information is constantly being fed to us, where all kinds of diets and different exercise regimes are being presented to us, with such a wide variety of choices, we can easily be confused. Eventually, we will feel frustrated because what we have tried is not working. We lurch awkwardly from one new thing to the next, from a diet to the gym, from detoxification to yoga, from spa treatments to the newest and trendiest exercise techniques, seeking the right formula.

We don't realize that while we are in this frantic search mode, trying to achieve a better or a perfect-looking body, we have forgotten how to move it properly and efficiently. We have lost that essential movement connection, that first spark that initiated our life. We have lost the essential body-mind connection that has guided our species and enabled us to survive for hundreds of thousands of years.

The physical body

The vehicle: It is not for me to explain to you the divinely perfect and yet intricate nature of our physical body. I am not here, either, to deliver an anatomy lecture. In this book, I will simply raise your awareness on how to manage this beautiful vehicle more efficiently, how to understand it and keep it at its optimum efficiency and in healthy and intelligent movement. I will provide some valuable information and tips on how to move in order to improve your daily lifestyle.

The body-mind connection

Our body is not a bag of muscles and bones with an expiry date. It is a beautiful creation capable of incredible, fluid motion. Every single cell and organ in our body has a role to play, and all our muscles are meant to be used and moved in unison. **Our body is intelligent**. In order to connect to that innate body intelligence, we need body and mind to work together.

A long time ago, Eastern cultures understood this important principle; they created disciplines such as yoga, tai chi, and martial arts. For thousands of years, people in the East practised these methods of exercise based on the connection of the body and mind with great dedication and amazing results.

The Romans used to say *"MENS SANA IN CORPORE SANO"* to express what they thought of as an ideal, a healthy mind in a healthy body. That says it all! But over the years, and mainly within the last century, especially in Western cultures, we have forgotten about this connection, this perfect cooperation between BODY & MIND. In our modern society, we have lost that balance. We have learned to use our mind as our primary tool for survival. Sadly, we have forgotten about our perfect vehicle, our body.

Then one day, with horror, we realize that this perfect vehicle is getting rusty. Even worse, it no longer moves smoothly. What do we do? We need to reconnect the Mind and the Body; one can't be without the other.

IT ALL STARTS IN OUR BRAIN

You can have the best Ferrari car, but what is the point of having it if you are not a good driver?

Our brain is the ultimate Formula 1 driver of our vehicle, the Body.

When people ask why my Body ID Method works, I simply reply, because I make you use your brain when you exercise. It's all about creating beneficial patterns in the body, and it all starts from our Brain....

How does it work?

Let's talk neuroscience. I will be very short, simple and to the point. But this is essential information. This is the ultimate body-mind connection.

The basis of this will be the communication between brain cells, called neurons, and the resulting cellular changes that happen to create new movement patterns, or what we call "Muscle memory". This communication between our brain and our body happens all the time while we are not even aware of it.

Neurons communicate with each other by releasing chemical messengers known as neurotransmitters across a space between them called a synapse (A **synapse** is the point of communication between two neurons). This will eventually lead to, for example, new skills or even new movements.

If a synapse is not regularly used, it will deteriorate. As an analogy, if you don't practise a language, you will get rusty. The same is true in the body; for example, if a pianist doesn't practise the piano diligently, their skill will also deteriorate. The same will be true for a dancer or an athlete. The opposite is obviously also the case… **After all, practice makes perfect.**

We can harness the amazing capabilities of the body to learn new skills.

On a cellular level, this learning is known as neural plasticity; the more one brain cell communicates with another, the more receptors are recruited to the cell's membrane, which means that it is more likely for those receptors to bind with the neurotransmitters and produce an effect in the second neuron. All this means, basically, that the more receptors there are the more likely is that those two neurons will communicate again in the future.

A new habit is forming in your brain. The more this connection is utilized through new movement patterns, the stronger it will become. Eventually it will become the new normal and take over as a new and improved default mode. By training diligently and thoughtfully, any new pattern can be reprogrammed into the brain.

Through intelligent exercise training you too can utilise the ingenious gifts your body has to offer. After all… it all starts in our Brain…

HOW TO RECONNECT

The Ferrari analogy

Get the driving license for your vehicle, the BODY.

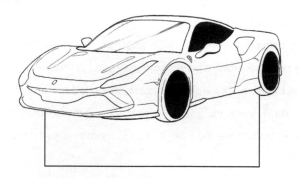

In order to teach people how to reconnect with their body I love using the Ferrari car analogy. You need to become the Formula 1 driver of your vehicle, learn to know it and control it, and finally be able to live a happy, healthy, long life while enjoying a beautiful ride.

THE FERRARI

When I see a client for the first time, I like to compare their body to a beautiful Formula 1 car. It is easy for everybody to relate to, especially if you are a driver, or like me if you love beautiful Italian cars.

Not many people are interested in discussing muscles and anatomy; actually, most of my clients enjoy it when I compare our body to a gorgeous sports car, I see an immediate interest and a big smile on their faces.

Of course, being Italian I like to relate to a beautiful red Ferrari, but please feel free to imagine your favourite model and colour. Yes, this is exactly what we are like when we first come from the manufacturer, a beautifully designed and perfectly engineered vehicle!

When young we run it at its full potential; it roars, it runs fast. We have all experienced that elation of being so wonderfully in control of our body and so free in our movements; the Ferrari runs so smoothly!

As we grow older, a few bumps and maybe a few accidents later, we forget to fine-tune our vehicle. By the time we reach our 40s we start to feel it does not run as smoothly as it used to, and eventually, we start complaining of some aches and pains. The beautiful engine is no longer roaring as it used to, it starts stalling, and it gets harder to drive.

Due to a different lifestyle, we have no more time to take our Ferrari for a ride, or to take it back regularly to the workshop for fine-tuning. And even if sometimes we find the time, it does not run as smoothly as it used to. Sad and frustrated, some of us will go to the extreme of parking it and letting it rust until it is forgotten, where it will eventually break down. I have not yet seen anyone abandoning his/her highly priced Ferrari car, but I do see every day in my practice people who have abandoned the most important vehicle of all, THEIR BODY.

In this manual, I would like to teach you how to retake control of your beautiful Ferrari, to become that skilled Formula 1 driver again, in control of your perfect roaring vehicle.

Remember that you used to be one. Yes, you were born to be that Formula 1 driver. Look at our ancestors; for hundreds of thousands of years they ran it and skilfully used it at its optimum potential. They were in full control of it. They ran it to survive, to fight, to hunt, to reproduce, to migrate, to protect their families and to build their homes; the engine was always roaring, the vehicle running, until the end of their lives. The vehicle served its purpose perfectly.

That memory is still in your body, imprinted in your cells' memory, you simply have not practised it. Let's get that manufacturer's manual and read it again.

How to do it?

THE KEY – breathing

First of all, in order to drive your Ferrari, you will need a **key. A magic key!**
This key will create that electrical connection that will turn the engine on, make it start up.

That magic key in our body **is BREATHING.** Yes, it is that simple.

Breathing is the main movement facilitator; breathing is the start-up of your vehicle.

Finally, **breathing** will initiate your vehicle, creating the perfect connection to your engine, **the core muscles.**

So being aware of the way we breathe, using the full potential of our lungs, is more than important that you may think; in fact, I would say it's vital. We will explore this in more depth in Chapter 6, THE IMPORTANCE OF BREATHING. I will teach you how to be aware of your breathing and use it as the perfect key to initiate your vehicle.

THE ENGINE, the core of the vehicle

To run our Ferrari we need, of course, a powerful engine. Once we have made the connection and inserted the key the engine will turn on and it will be ready to start running. Yes, that engine is the core of our vehicle, strong and efficient. Without it, the car will not run. It is the same for the human body; **the core muscles are our engine**.

A strong and efficient core is the secret that enables a body to move with optimum functionality, just like the Ferrari engine. And just like an engine, the core of our body has to be run regularly, checked, and fine-tuned by the finest engineers and workshop experts.

We will explore this more in Chapter 9, THE CORE ISSUE. I will teach you there how to understand the way your core muscles work and how to optimize your movement with a strong and supporting engine.

The Formula 1 Driver

We might have the most beautiful and efficient vehicle, the most expensive and latest Ferrari model, but if we do not know how to drive it properly it would be only a waste.

We need to be that skilful Formula 1 driver who is in full control of the vehicle, as well as a responsible and loving owner who takes good care of it when he is not driving it. I always say to my clients: Do not worry, during this process I will be sitting next to you, I will be your co-pilot and assist you during this reconnecting journey. But don't forget you are the driver!

THE VEHICLE

Some of us, especially if you are my age, have driven non-automatic cars. In countries such as Italy, most of the drivers, still today, even the young ones, prefer to drive using the old-fashioned manual gearbox. And even if you are not familiar with it, most of us understand that when we insert the key and turn the engine on our vehicle has to be in NEUTRAL, in parking position. It is only from this neutral position that we can move into the proper gear that will allow us to move our vehicle forwards, backwards, and finally change the speed from a slow walking pace to fast running. It is the same for our own perfect vehicle, the BODY.

The GEARBOX of our vehicle is our pelvis.

To run it efficiently it needs to be started from **a Neutral Position**, what we call a **neutral pelvis-spine position**.

Correct VEHICLE alignment = optimal performance.

Another essential element for a good driver is to make sure that his or her vehicle is kept always in optimum condition, and in perfect alignment.

Every part of the vehicle, engine, gearbox, wheels and suspension, has to work efficiently to give us optimal performance.

This is the role of POSTURE in our body.

An aligned posture is the only way to run our vehicle smoothly and efficiently; the more aligned, the better tuned, the more we can increase and optimize our performance.

In Chapter 7, POSTURE PERFECT, I will explain to you how to understand and maintain that neutral posture-pelvis position that will allow you, the driver, to run your vehicle efficiently.

And let's not forget the wheels and the tyres of our vehicle, legs and feet. If the legs/wheels are not in alignment they will interfere with the vehicle's performance. And if the tyres/feet are flat they will also limit the mechanical response of your vehicle.

THE KEY, breathing

THE ENGINE, the core muscles

THE GEARBOX, the pelvis

THE ALIGNMENT, the posture:

Your knees, the suspension

Your legs, the wheels

Your feet, the tyres

Combined with a skilful DRIVER,

YOU...

...will make your vehicle run at its maximum potential and efficiency, just as our ancestors did.

I tell my clients, and I repeat it to you, my readers, my role is simply to be your CO-PILOT. I will give you the tools and guide you through the process of re-learning what you knew but have forgotten. I will teach you to be that skilful Formula 1 driver again and take full control of your own vehicle.

Be patient and trust your intelligent body. It will provide you with the perfect vehicle for your journey of rediscovery of a healthy lifestyle in Movement.

Let's start the ride!

These feet are made for walking....

Walking is the best exercise you can do. It's easy, it's accessible to everyone and it's free.

Walk as much as you can; it's wonderful! I have learned that my feet are my wheels, and they can take me everywhere.

The incredible benefits of walking

Walking gives you a lot of benefits, and if it's done correctly and efficiently, it can be considered a very effective form of exercise. We all know that a good walk, especially in nature, does wonder for your health and for your mental well-being. A 30- to 45-minute daily walk can have several benefits:

- *It can improve your general fitness, and cardiac health.*

- *It alleviates depression and improves your mood.*

- *It can help you manage your weight.*

- *It improves your circulation.*

- *It will help you to maintain a healthy posture.*

- *It is a low-impact form of exercise, it will not damage your knees and your back, and it can be done for long periods of time.*

But what I have found to be one of the most fascinating of all facts on the benefits of walking, comes from the research study from Stanford University on **"divergent thinking"**. According to the study, "walking opens up the free flow of ideas" and can increase your creative thoughts by an average of 60 per cent. Now I understand why the best ideas come to me during my walks!

Apparently, I am not the only one; Ludwig van Beethoven fed his creativity by going on long daily walks in nature, where he felt the most inspired to create his symphonies. He used to carry with him a notebook and a pencil to write his music while walking in the woods.

I carry my iPhone, and I voice-record many of my ideas while walking; then, when I get back home, I put them down in writing. Many of the chapters in this book came to me as an inspiration during my daily afternoon walk in my beautiful local park.

And what better title for Stanford University's research than *"Give Your Ideas Some Legs"?*

(*Give Your Ideas Some Legs: The Positive Effect of Walking on Creative Thinking* – Marily Oppezzo and Daniel L. Schwartz, Stanford University)

WALKING VS RUNNING

Today there is strong scientific evidence that confirms the benefits of walking as part of your fitness routine. A brisk walk can be as effective as running.

Clinical research has proven that walking is just as good as running when it comes to lowering your risk for heart disease. For instance, a 15-minute jog burns about the same number of calories as a 30-minute brisk walk. The advantage of walking is that it is low-impact exercise, which makes it safer than running. Running, on the other hand, is high-impact exercise, due to the vigorous pounding of your feet on the surface; this makes it more challenging for your back and knees; therefore, it can cause injuries. Every day during my daily walk in the park I see joggers struggling with their posture. It hurts my eyes seeing these people panting and making so much effort while carrying their body so inefficiently. They are the ones at great risk of injuries.

WHEN RUNNING IS BEST

I advise running as part of your fitness routine if you are practising sports which require great endurance, speed and stamina, including football, rugby, basketball, racket sports such as tennis, or if you are training for a triathlon or a marathon. Remember; to run your vehicle, your body efficiently, and maximize your performance, you need to maintain a good posture alignment.

MY TIPS

- Start using the commute to work as your daily workout. Walk to work and maximize that precious time when you can use your vehicle and keep it running.

- Increase your walking performance slowly.

- When you use public transport to work or to any destination, come out a couple of stops before and walk. Allow your body to get used to walking by increasing the distance. You may be surprised at how efficient it can be.

- If you have to drive to work, try to park your car at least 20 to 30 minutes away from your work and use that distance to walk.

- I know the weather can be a nuisance. Too cold and rainy or too hot and humid; well, I can assure you once you are well equipped and have the engine running you will not feel it.

- Invest in a perfectly fitting and comfortable pair of shoes, good tyres for your wheels, that will give you the ideal plantar support (support the arches of your feet); this will also facilitate a better posture alignment. Ladies forget walking on those killer stilettos. I agree, they look good, so do what I do every day; put them in your bag and wear them when you get to work, or just before that meeting or a special date. You will have saved your poor feet the damage and discomfort of high heels.

- Make sure that when you are walking you are not carrying a heavy bag and, if you must carry one, alternate it from side to side or carry a well-designed backpack.

- The most important thing to remember when you walk is to create a steady rhythm and keep it going. It's best not to stop and try to maintain your pace without distractions. The speed should be moderate to brisk.

- Be aware of your breathing while you walk. Once you have learned the proper way to breathe (see Chapter 6, THE IMPORTANCE OF BREATHING), use it to optimize your daily walk.

- You will enjoy it more and more and, eventually, as I do, you will rediscover how much easier and more efficient it is to walk everywhere... and you can get inspired too...

PAOLO'S STORY

A True Transformation;
it's never too late...

Paolo is a very charming Italian man and the CEO of a big worldwide company. He was introduced to me by a doctor friend who was treating him for the chronic pain he had been suffering for many years in the lower back, knees and ankles. When I first met him, Paolo was 49, in pain, and, in his own words; I was his last hope.

This is Paolo's story:

When he was a young man Paolo had been a very successful student and was a professional athlete at university, a true star.

At that time Paolo suffered some sports injuries, nothing major or particularly significant. His injuries were not taken much into consideration at the time as Paolo had a very athletic build, and a beautiful, naturally strong body.

However, as the years passed, with marriage, children and career, Paolo's active life ground to a halt. No more sports, no more exercise routines except for an occasional game of golf. Paolo's old injuries started to reappear with a vengeance. The hectic lifestyle of a high-profile businessman, half of which was spent sitting at his desk and half in an aeroplane flying from country to country around the world, combined with a total lack of appropriate exercise, had finally taken its toll. His pain had become unmanageable, his posture greatly compromised, and his walk had a very pronounced limp due to an old foot injury that had not healed properly.

During the last couple of years prior to our meeting, Paolo had tried everything, from all kinds of therapies to different kinds of personal training. Nothing had worked, and his entire body was deteriorating at an alarming rate. Paolo now had serious difficulty going up and down stairs and getting in and out of the car; he could no longer go for walks and had to stop playing his favourite sport, golf, altogether.

Though Paolo was naturally strong and beautifully built, at 49 he looked older than his age. He had lost that sparkle.

When I saw Paolo for his postural assessment, I realized that the main challenge with him was time. He was travelling extensively. He was never in any one country for any length of time. How could I create a programme suitable for him while he was hopping from place to place like a grasshopper?

I looked at his movement personality, and at his build. I knew that I could find a way to help him.

Being the athletic body type, naturally strong and proportionally built, was an advantage. But best of all Paolo had that kind of committed personality, a sense of discipline which, later in the programme, would help him enormously.

Having been an athlete during his youth and involved in competitive sports was also an advantage. Paolo knew what discipline was. His body remembered. I simply had to guide him to find that connection again.

When we started our first session it was as if his body had been unplugged from his mind. There was no connection between muscles and movement, and he could not breathe efficiently. His entire posture had adapted to a bad alignment. One side of the body was dominating and doing all the work; it was overly used and stressed, while the other side was so disconnected that some of the muscles in the leg were starting to atrophy.

This imbalance was causing him to have a very noticeable limp, and of course compromising his entire movement functionality.

During my first sessions with Paolo, I felt like a skilful electrician. I was slowly reconnecting the fine cables between the body, the muscles and the mind.

Paolo was amazing, responsive and focused, and always participated with enthusiasm in this reconnecting process.

I knew from the beginning that because of that discipline and natural positive commitment Paolo would heal in a few months. I started by using Pilates-based exercises with the Reformer (the Pilates Reformer is a spring resistance exercise machine created by Joseph Pilates). That helped him to realign his body while working on deep muscle strengthening. Breathing was a big challenge for Paolo; he had to retrain that lost lung capacity. We worked intensively on it. Once he saw and felt the dramatic changes in his body, after only a few sessions, he became even more motivated.

I designed a special personalized programme for him. I would see Paolo regularly, almost on a daily basis during the time he was in town (about 10 to 15 days a month). The rest of the time he would practise the exercise programme I had created for him on his own, using the tools and the necessary props I had provided for him. Very simple but effective exercise routines.

His strong sense of discipline, accompanied by the right choice of movements, was the main factor contributing to his fast and very successful recovery.

Within three months the change in his body started to be very evident. It was amazing! Paolo was very excited; the changes were now also visible to his family and close friends. Paolo seemed to have found his vigour again. He looked happier and younger.

Within a year his limp had disappeared. He could move freely and easily going up and down the stairs of his beautiful home. He was enjoying long walks and once again he was able to play golf.

Eventually, he had to change his entire wardrobe; none of his old clothes would fit him anymore, his figure was now trimmed and toned. He certainly looked much younger than his age.

After two years of practising my BODY ID programme, the change was dramatic. Paolo was looking at his best, strong, fit and healthy. Paolo is still seeing me regularly up until today and has become a master of his own body.

Recently, Paolo celebrated his 60th birthday looking handsome, fit and healthy. For Paolo, just like me, the 50s were the beginning of a new and exciting phase of his life. This new movement awareness will be with Paolo forever. He is enjoying this second phase of his life with his regained youthful vigour as much as he enjoyed his youth.

When I called Paolo to wish him a happy birthday and congratulate him on his wonderful appearance, Paolo thanked me, stating that his new body and great energy most definitely were due to my programme and me.

What a joy and what a gift!

BODY
Types

Beauty in nature comes in all different shapes, sizes and colours, and so it is for the human body.

Throughout history, the concept of beauty has changed and adapted. Artists, trendsetters and fashion designers have decreed the new canons of beauty. We should not be dictated to by the aesthetic rules of today's stereotypes. We can't possibly be the picture-perfect figures that we see in magazines, which have been artistically retouched and modified by special photo applications. We should instead celebrate our diversity, the beauty and uniqueness of our bodies, and make the best of what Mother Nature has given us. **Different BODY SHAPES!**

Our genetic imprint, our race and our lifestyle, they all define and determine this uniqueness and make us different from everyone else. Geographically we belong to different places and races and we carry different characteristics and genetic imprints.

We also need to consider that the beauty canons might vary accordingly to different traditions and cultural beliefs. What might be considered attractive in one culture might not be considered so in another one. We need to acknowledge those differences, accept them, understand them and finally learn how to make the best of our genetic features.

A wrong lifestyle, or a badly treated injury, or simply having neglected our body, might have led us to a point of our life where we hardly recognize ourselves, and we wonder how that beautiful, strong, and healthy body we were born with has vanished or deteriorated.

The simple truth is we can easily regain that body:

AT ANY AGE, AT ANY TIME.

We just need to keep the body in movement, the right movement. We need to choose the most appropriate activities, fitness and movement programmes, specifically tailored to suit our BODY TYPE.

DIFFERENT BODIES, DIFFERENT PERSONALITIES, DIFFERENT EXERCISES

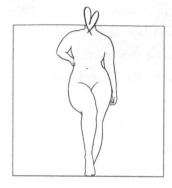

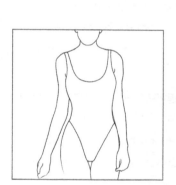

How to choose the right exercise regime for your unique body?

Have you noticed how much attention is given to the variety of styles and special cuts of jeans, trousers, shirts and dresses that might be most suitable to enhance our different body shapes nowadays? As we look at this wide variety of choices, how many of us wonder what would best enhance our figure?

The same attention is being focused on diets. Some of us are meat eaters; others are vegans or vegetarians; many have specific food allergies or intolerances to certain foods. We automatically expect that this information will be taken into consideration when designing an adequate diet to suit our personal dietary needs.

Think of the exercise programme just like a diet suited to your personal needs.

THE RIGHT FOOD FOR YOUR MUSCLES

We use all the information available to us in order to personalize a diet to our specific needs. So why don't we apply the same principle to a physical regime? Why don't we recognize that each person and each body type need a different exercise regime and a different approach?

Back in history (2000-1500 BCE), Ayurvedic medicine, originating in India, recognized these body differences and categorized the human body into three distinct "Doshas" or body types.

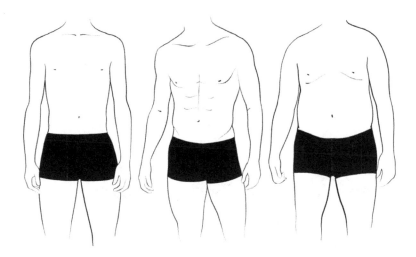

- *Vata, the slim type*

- *Pitta, the athletic type*

- *Kapha, the voluptuous/strongly built type*

These names recognize and describe the differences in each body type; in physical traits and personality traits; and enable healthcare and other professionals to advise on appropriate diets, and even suitable exercises, particularly yoga asanas.

Ideally, in order to create a healthy balance in our lives, we should balance all the three different elements of the Ayurvedic Doshas:

air for Vata, fire for Pitta, and earth for Kapha.

Some people might have the characteristics of a single dominant body type, as in my case, and many others might carry the physical appearance of a body type and the traits of the personality of another one. That is why it is so important to understand our nature when designing a specific and personalized programme.

The same theory of different body types was promoted by Dr William H. Sheldon (1898-1977) in the 1940s, when he introduced the three body types to the modern world. William Sheldon was an American psychologist who spent his life observing the variety of human bodies. He categorized the human body into three different types:

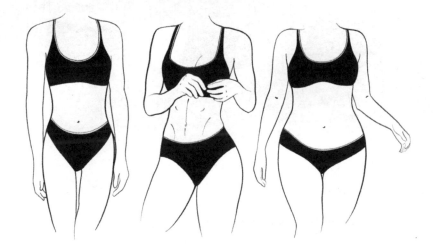

Ectomorph, Mesomorph, Endomorph.

These three categories matched the three Ayurvedic doshas.

- *Ectomorph = Vata = slim*

- *Mesomorph = Pitta = athletic*

- *Endomorph = Kapha = voluptuous/strongly built*

Of course, people come in all different shapes. But most of us can be placed into one of these body type categories. Sometimes we carry mixed characteristics belonging to two different body types. I am sure you will recognize yourself in one or more of them.

Today we call them all different names, the apple shape, the pear shape, for example, we also have differentiations bases on our glandular activities, called glandular body types.

Mine is a user-friendly and simple summary on how to identify your body type and the most appropriate exercise regime for your particular body type. I have personally added one element to it, your **movement personality.** This will help you to identify even better what kind of "mover" you are. Each Body Type has a different movement personality, and this is where I will be focusing, advising you on which kind of exercise regime will suit you best.

THE SKINNY TYPE – VATA – ECTOMORPH

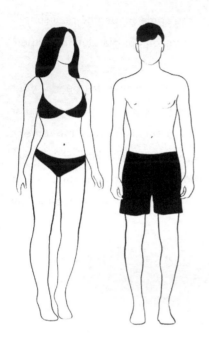

Physical traits:

- *Thin, delicately built, lean.*

- *Lightly muscled.*

- *Takes longer to gain muscle.*

Personality traits:

- *Creative, mentally quick, talks and moves quickly.*

- *Excitable, lively and fun-loving.*

- *Can easily stress.*

- *Irregular in daily routines; has high energy but in short bursts*

The skinny type – Vata – Ectomorph's physique is a fragile and delicate one.

It is relatively linear in shape, with narrow hips and pelvis, and long arms and legs. The muscles and bone outlines are usually visible, and normally have less fat and muscle mass than people with other body types. They are the lucky ones who don't put on weight easily. Their primary concern is their frail stature, consisting of small bones and joints that have the tendency to be injured easily during sports activities. These body types are not naturally strong and if they want to improve their muscle definition they will have to work intelligently and with appropriate effort in order to avoid injuries.

The skinny body type needs less exercise than the other body types, so lighter activities and low-impact exercises such as yoga,

Pilates, walking and swimming are the most suitable ones. At the same time, having long, lean muscles, they don't bulk easily. This body type can benefit also from some cardio and weight resistance exercises to improve stamina and lack of muscle definition. Endurance is not their forte, so they have to be very careful when performing aerobic and high-impact activities and take these in smaller doses.

When putting on weight, the body fat distribution in this body type is mainly distributed on the lower part of the body, hips and thighs, especially in the female body. An appropriate exercise programme will have to focus and target these areas and activate blood circulation in the legs.

I often see personal trainers pushing people belonging to this body type too hard, and not taking into consideration their fragile nature and lack of endurance. I advise them to keep cardio and high-impact exercise moderate and under professional supervision.

Movement personality: Active to hyperactive

In terms of movement personality, the skinny type – Vata – is very motivated, active and creative, with a tendency to become hectic and hyperactive. This body type can get also very easily stressed and tense.

People who belong to this type need activities that are more calming to suit their very excitable and hyperactive nature.

They are the ones who like to exercise the most but, oddly enough, they are the ones who least need it!

The Right Equation

The advice I give to this body type is to exercise with consistency. Two to three exercise sessions a week are sufficient if kept regular.

The exercises I advise for this body type are:

Low-impact exercises that stimulate BODY-MIND connection such as:

- **Pilates**
- **Gyrotonic**®
- **Yoga**
- **Dance to stimulate their creativity**
- **Walking**

As this personality tends to be hyperactive, stressed, and also quite scatty, these kinds of exercises will keep them focused and stimulate their curious intellectual nature.

Pilates

Pilates is very suited to this body type movement personality, especially if they wish to get some strength and muscle definition. It's also very safe, as it can be modified to very specific needs and different age groups, from post-rehabilitation purposes to pre/post-natal, to general body conditioning. The safety aspect of Pilates is good for this body type, which can have quite a fragile nature and tendency to injure easily.

Yoga

Yoga is very good to pacify this body type's wandering minds, to reduce their stress and calm their excitable nature.

Gyrotonic®

For flexibility, coordination, and strengthening; it can also be sport-specific, especially for golfers, dancers, gymnasts and swimmers.

OUTDOOR ACTIVITIES

Walking

A good outdoor walk will calm their nature and pacify their busy mind. This is probably the best activity for the hectic Vata type.

Swimming

Outdoor activities should not be performed in winter as this body type reacts badly to the cold.

Moderate Cardio

Being lithe, creative and bouncy by nature, the skinny type will benefit most from aerobic activities such as dancing, or brisk walks.

Gym, running and high impact sports should be experienced in very small doses and with professional guidance. I normally advise this only to elite movers, such as professional sportspeople who have to maintain a higher level of strength and endurance in physical activities.

Dosage (amount of exercise)

Light to moderate, two to three times a week, and most of all **in regular doses.**

I often see these body types overdosing on exercise for a considerable length of time or, alternatively, going through periods of no exercise at all. This is typical of their scatty personality. This is also one reason they injure so easily.

It is imperative to place these body types in the right environment, where they will thrive.

THE ATHLETIC TYPE – PITTA – MESOMORPH

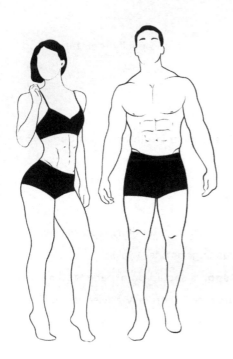

Physical traits

- *Medium physique, strong and well built, generally carries quite naturally good posture*

- *More of a rectangular shape, with strong arms and legs, muscular body*

- *Gains muscle easily*

- *Can gain fat.*

- *When putting on weight this type will easily accumulate body fat, mainly in the middle of the body and not so much in the limbs.*

Personality traits

- *Sharp mind.*

- *Good concentration and focused.*

- *Competitive, enjoys challenges.*

Typical A personality

The Athletic type has well-defined muscles and large bones. Arms and legs are developed and have good muscle definition. Their strong build can easily take challenging physical activities. They make excellent athletes, however sometimes they tend to have more drive than endurance. They gain muscle mass very easily. That is why they need a moderate amount of high-impact exercise in order to avoid excess bulk. Women belonging to this body type have to be especially careful if they do not want to gain too much bulk and lose a more feminine body shape.

If out of shape, this body type will accumulate fat mainly in the middle part of the body, the trunk, while the limbs will remain quite unchanged and with relatively good muscle tone.

A suitable programme should focus on appropriate **cardio, and core exercises**. Legs and arms are naturally strong and well defined, so lengthening exercises would be ideal. I see often the opposite, some personal trainers giving this body type unsuitable exercises, which will result in excessive bulk in the entire body.

Movement personality

Active and competitive.

The athletic type loves a challenge. They are very competitive by nature and enjoy mainly outdoor activities and many competitive sports (such as swimming, running, skiing, and tennis). They are very disciplined; you will see them running in the park at 6 am or religiously following their gym routines.

In order to avoid excessive bulk in their body, they have to maintain a balance with more low-impact exercises.

Because they are so disciplined and focused, and physically suited, most competitive/target-orientated athletes belong to this body type group.

THE RIGHT EQUATION

The exercise regime I advise for this group is a combination of high- and low-impact exercises:

A combination of cardiovascular exercises and sports routines.

This will facilitate the fat burning process as they tend to put body fat on around the abdomen.

For ladies who want to avoid excess body bulk, I advise avoiding heavy weights and too much high-impact exercise.

Along with:

Pilates

For strengthening, toning and lengthening. Very suitable for any sport-specific programmes, to enhance sports performance or rehabilitate after a sports injury.

Yoga or power yoga

For strength, flexibility, and mind relaxation.

Gyrotonic®

For flexibility, coordination, and strengthening.

Sport specific, especially for golfers, dancers, gymnasts and swimmers.

All the above methods will improve the Athletic body type while toning and lengthening their muscles.

Gym

Cardiovascular training is very important for this body type, as their tendency is to put fat in the middle part of their body, the core. If you have a weak back or sensitive knees, I advise using the elliptical cross trainer rather than the treadmill, for 30 to 40 minutes, three times a week. It is safer for the knees, being less high-impact.

A lightweight training programme is advised, especially for the ladies, as the muscles can bulk very easily.

Outdoor activities

Walking, power walking, gentle jogging, swimming, all kinds of sports are very suitable for this body type as they enjoy very much outdoor and competitive activities.

Dosage (amount of exercise)

Depending on their fitness level.

Moderate to heavy, three to five times a week.

THE VOLUPTUOUS/STRONGLY BUILT – KAPHA – ENDOMORPH

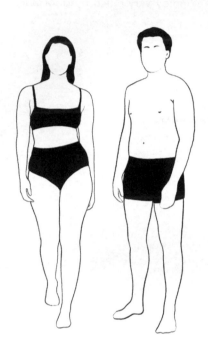

Physical traits

- *Soft body, round physique.*

- *For the ladies, very sensual hourglass figure.*

- *Gains weight easily, can gain muscle easily.*

- *Tendency to retain liquids.*

- *Very good physical endurance.*

- *These body types have a very strong constitution and steady energy, but often lack agility owing to the tendency to carry excess weight.*

- *When putting on weight, this body type will accumulate body fat equally over the whole body, upper, middle and lower.*

- *They are the body type most suited for all exercises, as long as they maintain a limber and relatively light body.*

Personality traits

- *Easy going*

- *Calm, focused, and relaxed*

- *Slow moving*

Movement Personality: Sedentary

People with strongly built body types are the best suited for physical endurance as they have the natural build for high-endurance sports and activities. Unfortunately, this body type personality tends to be quite complacent towards exercise and sports. They need more exercise than the other body types in order to burn their excess body fat.

THE RIGHT EQUATION

The exercise regime I advise for this group is:

All activities are good for this strong, high-endurance physique.

The more they move the better.

Cardio, aerobic exercises and sports; anything that makes them move and sweat.

Pilates, **Gyrotonic®**, yoga can be the perfect complement to the regime, maintaining a balance between high- and low-impact exercise.

Gym

Like the Pitta body type, cardiovascular training is very important for this body type, due to their tendency to gain weight. I advise cardio exercise, for 30 to 40 minutes, three to five times a week.

A lightweight training programme is advised as the muscles in this body type can also bulk very easily. Ladies, please watch it!

For the best results, this body type should always have an instructor to encourage, push and motivate them in the right direction. They do not lack strength or stamina, but motivation.

Outdoor activities

Use your feet, and walk as much as you can, the more the better.

I do not advise running, especially if overweight; it could have a bad effect on the knees and other joints. Use a cross trainer/elliptical trainer at the gym instead.

Swimming, cycling and golf.

This body type does not much enjoy competitive sports.

Chose any outdoor activity of your liking.

Dosage (amount of exercise)

Depending on their fitness level

Moderate to heavy, from three to five times per week.

Understanding who you are

Once you have understood which body category you belong to it is easier to make a better choice on what is the most suitable exercise regime for your own body type.

My guidelines are directed mainly to a healthy person. If you suffer from any chronic pain or have been injured, you must seek health professional advice before undertaking any previously suggested exercise routines.

Obviously, elite movers such as athletes and professional dancers follow a much more stringent regime.

In order to obtain the best results, you should always tailor your exercise programme to the body type to which you belong. If you are practising a particular exercise regime that is not suited to your body type, you may not be seeing the results you have been expecting or might end up injured.

Men and women should have different exercise regimes simply because our bodies are built for different purposes (see Chapter 3, FROM CAVE TO CUBICLE). As I mentioned at the beginning of the book, the human body was created to survive in the harsh environment of the natural elements. The woman/female's main purpose was to reproduce by carrying the babies, giving birth and nurturing the children, while the man/male would hunt and provide and protection to the family.

EXERCISE

Now that you have decided which body type you belong to and have a clearer idea about your movement personality, list what kind of activities would suit you the best in order to have a balanced exercise regime. Take a piece of paper or notebook, and write as follows:

Choose one high-impact activity, e.g. sport, gym, running....

Choose one low-impact activity, e.g. Pilates, yoga, walking ....

Now write how much time per week you will dedicate to your healthy movement plan.

Even one hour is good enough, especially if combined with a daily walk.

I do not want to hear, "Sorry, I am too busy; I do not have time," it is just an excuse. Everyone can get one or two hours a week free.

TATYANA'S STORY

The Skinny Body Type – Vata/Ectomorph

My dear friend Tatyana is simply gorgeous.

She has the looks and the body of a top model, tall and blonde, with killer legs that, when she puts on a mini skirt, can stop the traffic.

So... you might think, what has this long-legged top model, beautiful Tatyana, got to do with this book? What more does she need than what a generous Mother Nature has given her?

Here is her story; all too easily, this could be you. Tatyana had chosen an exercise regime quite wrong for her body type.

When she came to see me for a postural assessment, Tatyana complained that she was too thin and that she kept losing weight and was very tired. Despite her daily routine at the local gym where she spent an hour running, her muscles were not toned. She looked rather emaciated.

Tatyana was exhausted, too thin, and after fainting at the gym during her daily work out, her doctor had advised her to stop exercising altogether.

Looking at Tatyana, I had to agree with her. She was too thin and her muscles were too weak, they did not have any tone or definition.

The programme she had chosen at the gym was definitely not suitable for her body type.

Tatyana's muscles were long and thin. They did not bulk as easily as those of the other body types. The more she tried, the more exhausted she got. Tatyana was a perfect example of the skinny body type. She needed a programme where she did not exhaust herself by running every day and using a high-impact gym routine. She could not afford to lose any weight because she did not have, lucky her, any excess body fat. She needed to work on strengthening and toning the muscles while building some stamina. Also, due to her fragile frame, Tatyana could very easily have been injured.

A combination of gentle, intelligent, low-impact exercises and Pilates was the perfect exercise regime for her, and no more than three times per week. She could work on resistance-based exercises, strengthening the muscles while not exhausting her body, and building some good muscle definition.

I advised Tatyana to start with a gentler regime, focusing on low-impact strengthening exercises. Pilates was a very suitable exercise regime.

I remember Tatyana struggling at the beginning of her programme, for though she had been going to the gym every day, she was very weak. She was struggling as she was trying to control her movements; her balance and stability were very poor, and she had very weak core muscles. However, with my guidance, she thrived. Three months later her body had transformed into a stronger and beautifully toned shape.

Tatyana was no longer losing weight. She looked healthy and fit, and those killer legs looked better than ever. Most important of all, Tatyana was no longer exhausted all the time and she had found a perfectly balanced exercise routine that best suited her needs and body type.

GEORGIA'S STORY

The Athletic Body Type – Pitta/Mesomorph

Georgia came to me as a client when I still had my first studio in my Tropical Eden in Singapore.

She had heard that my new method had finally arrived in Singapore and was curious to try it.

She was attending the gym diligently every day, but to her great disappointment and frustration her body kept changing and, unfortunately, not for the better; she was getting heavier and bulkier.

Georgia had a typical, strong athletic body.

After a couple of years of weight training and energetic high-impact aerobic exercises advised with great enthusiasm by her personal trainer, Georgia's body had transformed into a considerably less feminine and appealing shape. She looked bulky and heavy. She had gained weight and did not fit comfortably into her clothes. She also complained that her upper body looked like a bodybuilder. She dreamed of having a beautiful, swan-like neckline that would make her look elegant and feminine.

Georgia came to me crying for help. "Why?" she said, "The more I work out, the worse it gets. I work so hard. I go to the gym every day. My personal trainer pushes me and I do as he says. What am I doing wrong? What is wrong with my body?"

I knew in a single glance what the problem was. Georgia had a strong, sturdy frame. She was the perfect personification of the Athletic body type.

Her muscles were short and had a tendency to bulk up. The more she practised weight training, running and bicycling the more she increased her muscle mass and therefore her total body bulk.

There was absolutely nothing wrong with her body; she was just doing the wrong exercise routines.

Georgia needed a different programme. She needed exercises that would challenge her body in a very different way. Her muscles needed to be elongated and stretched as they were toned. She needed to find the right balance and the right amount of body effort. She needed to work more in lengthening and flexibility while doing some appropriate strengthening and cardiovascular training. She never needed to work so hard. Her muscles had increased too much in volume and she felt very uncomfortable with her body shape.

I asked Georgia to stop doing what she was doing. No more gym, weight training, running and sweating. She needed a complete break. Her muscles needed a holiday.

She looked at me in horror. "Oh no! If I stop I will get fat, and unfit. How can you ask me to do this?"

I talked to Georgia about her body type. I explained about her movement personality. I told her that the exercises she was doing were most unsuitable for her body. The more she worked out at the gym, especially with a weight training programme, the bulkier and heavier she would get.

I convinced her to give me three months and to try to work with me two to three times a week. I wanted her body to have a rest, her muscles to become longer and leaner and for her to become more feminine in shape.

*I designed a special programme that best suited her. I used a combination of exercises to give her control and resistance while lengthening the muscles, and **Gyrotonic®** exercises to challenge her body by using weights in a pulley system; this way she would not bulk up her muscles. I worked* *on her posture realignment, which had been compromised by years of the wrong exercise routines. She would then go for a good power walk three times a week in the beautiful botanical gardens in Singapore. Due to the extreme heat and humidity, I advised her to do it in the early evenings. The advantage of living in such a climate is that a good 30- to 40-minute fast walk, as well as improved fitness, also gives you the benefits of a good sweat, if not of a sauna. This was just what Georgia needed.*

Georgia trusted me. She stopped her harsh gym exercise routines and within three months, as I had promised, Georgia had lost one full clothes size and now had a beautiful swan-like neckline. She looked beautiful and feminine.

ROSELLA'S STORY

The Voluptuous Body Type
– Kapha/Endomorph

Rosella arrived at my studio on a Harley-Davidson, dressed in full leathers, helmet under her arm, and her "comfortable baggy" clothes in a bag over her shoulder.

Her main concern was increasing pain and stiffness in her hips and knees, which she knew was being aggravated by a steady weight gain that she had been experiencing over the past five years but which no amount of "dieting" seemed to affect.

She looked hot and sweaty, tired and very uncomfortable. She admitted that my studio sent her into a panic as she actively avoided mirrors any larger than a compact mirror. She felt overweight and unattractive and was increasingly frustrated that her body was stopping her doing the physically active things she wanted to do.

Her once fit, healthy body, capable of rising to any challenge she chose, was ageing and bloating at an ever-accelerating rate. This worried her as she intended to continue to ride her Harley and participate in the outdoor activities that she enjoyed. After all, she had been born and bred in Outback Australia and had lived an active, outdoor-orientated lifestyle. She had switched from horse to Harley.

As we talked, she listed the things she had tried. Weight loss medication had never worked. All the well-known diet programmes had failed. At the gym, she had bulked up so much in six months that she had gone up two sizes in jeans and t-shirts as well as putting so much pressure on her knees that they hurt even more than before. Bike riding and rollerblading were too time consuming and a fall when rollerblading had left her unable to do any sort of exercise for more than six months. She added that aerobics classes left her feeling hopeless and exhausted as she jumped and bent beside cat-walk thin fashion-conscious bodies. And in her own colourful words, impersonating a pretzel at yoga classes had made standing up an act of torture.

Walking was not only too time consuming for her but extremely uncomfortable, given the tropical climate of Singapore, and the state of her knees and her weight.

She knew exercise was important to lead an efficient and pain-free lifestyle.

Rosella was the perfect example of the voluptuous body type. She needed a lot of physical activity, but the weight had become her enemy. She was caught in a typical Catch 22 situation. She could not exercise because of the excess weight she was carrying, and she could not lose weight because she could not exercise. After her latest injury, she had been finding it increasingly difficult to get on and off her motorcycle.

The first thing I suggested was that we attack her problem from both ends and break the vicious circle. As I designed a suitable and closely supervised exercise regime for her I recommended that she meet with a reputable nutritionist who would design a special diet suitable to her lifestyle, and body type.

I started working on Rosella's awareness. For her, being in a comfortable environment, without feeling judged about her looks, was the first step to her transformation. I created a safe environment where she felt comfortable, not too many mirrors around and no other people. I slowly reconnected her mind to her body and let her accept her body. I educated her on her body type and how to make the best of it. In the meantime, Rosella started to follow the recommendations of the nutritionist.

I worked on her alignment, which had been compromised after years of weight problems and lack of appropriate exercise. Pilates and very gentle cardio exercises were the perfect combination.

After a few months of following my regime Rosella had lost most of her extra weight. As she became lighter and leaner I challenged her more and more with cardio/endurance-orientated exercises. Rosella thrived.

Now when she walks into my studio in her leathers, she no longer looks hot and bothered, she looks hot and sexy.

Rosella – in her own words

My name is Rosella. One morning I lay in bed visualizing my exercise routine and being fit and healthy. I had been doing that a lot lately. I really wanted my health and fitness back but nothing I had done seemed to work. I hated feeling fat and ugly. I hated the fat clothes I was being forced to wear and I hated mirrors even more as they were an unpleasant illustration of what I had become. It was getting hard to feel cheerful and optimistic. And I was getting VERY tired of people asking me why I was so fat. One day I was going to ask them why they were so ugly/skinny? Visualizing a slimmer, healthy body didn't seem to be working either, even if it did give me an extra twenty minutes in bed.

I needed to do something serious about my body, fast, before it started affecting not only my social life but my work. I had never heard of Ivana Daniell, although I had heard of Pilates. Pilates, to the best of my knowledge, was for people who had been seriously injured and needed physiotherapy or who wanted to go to a group class and roll around the floor on a ball. My mother had fallen off one of those balls and really hurt her back. I was fairly sure I didn't want to do that.

A friend suggested that I meet her friend, Ivana, and gave me a number to call. I dutifully called and felt reassured by the pleasant reception I got, and the simple instructions for my first visit. A few days later, I dusted off my old gym clothes to change into, and off I went.

I was horrified when I stepped into the studio. It was light, bright and full of mirrors. One step more and I would have entered my worst nightmare. Fortunately for me, I was quietly greeted, gently walked through some forms and guided into a changing area blissfully free of mirrors. Then I met Ivana. If people believe in love at first sight, then it will be no hard thing to understand the instant rapport that sparked between us. It was trust and friendship at first sight.

Slim, graceful and glowing with energy, she was the first person in a long time who didn't instantly make me feel over-sized, clumsy and an ugly blot on the horizon. I didn't even notice the mirrors as we moved down to the talking corner. I experienced a few moments of apprehension as I took in the cushions but was soothed by the gentle and sincere direction of our conversation. I figured I would worry about how to get up later. I sank with as much grace as I could summon into the huge pile of cushions.

And embarked on a new phase in my life!

Ivana then explained to me that I belonged to the voluptuous body type. My being overweight for her was simply a sign of imbalance that could easily be fixed if I followed her directions.

No more lying in bed dreaming of exercising, just simple action. No excuses.

She had the perfect action plan for me. We started our first session learning to breathe properly, and she introduced me to the Pilates Reformer machine. As our sessions continued, I started to regain suppleness of movement. Soon I began to move more freely, and Ivana increased the level of challenge on the exercise machines exponentially so that my fitness began to increase more rapidly.

By following the guidelines of the dietician Ivana recommended and making educated choices, I changed my eating habits. By following Ivana's guidelines and learning to make educated choices, I changed my exercise regime, and within months could feel and see the incredible results.

These are three examples of the many success stories that I treasure. They are the reaffirmation of the application of my movement philosophy. This is where I experience the joy and the excitement in my work. In the next chapter, I will talk about the importance of maintaining good posture and go into more detail about movement personality and how to assess it.

The
IMPORTANCE
of Breathing

I constantly remind my clients that breathing is the most important act of life. It is our very first one, but unfortunately, it is the most undervalued. We take breathing for granted. Given how important it is to our well-being breathing should never be neglected.

Breathing is essential to our health.

Breathing will release us from stress and tension.

Breathing will also facilitate our movements, creating the right muscle connection.

Breathing will help you to support a correct posture.

Breathing will increase your energy.

Too often we underestimate the importance of breathing. Air, as much as food and water, contains essential elements for our survival. Few people realize how breathing can improve the quality of our lives and contribute to our health as much as proper eating does. **Proper breathing is nourishment for our cells.**

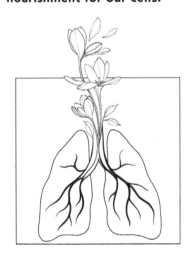

We take this natural miracle for granted. We breathe without thinking or putting any conscious effort into the process and without realizing that breathing is LIFE. Breathing brings oxygen into our bloodstream. Oxygen is the most important nutrient for our cells, for our heart, for our brain, and for our organs. Limiting our access to oxygen will affect our body in a negative way.

Breathing is also a powerful anti-stress agent. Observe what we do every time we are in a stressful situation, or we are tense and angry. Our breath becomes faster and very shallow, our heart rate increases, and our brain will produce cortisol, the stress hormone. By simply taking a few deep breaths, our heart rate will slow down, our bloodstream will get more oxygen, and our brain will receive the signal to relaaaaax... deep breathing also helps the production of endorphins, the "feel-good" chemicals.

Both my sons, Vinci and Chris, have heard me saying this since they were born. How sweet it was of them since they were young boys, every time they saw me stressed or upset, or a bit too excited in what they called "the Italian way" they would say, Mom, please take a deep breath... inhale... and... calm down... look at me and count 1... 2... 3... and relax. Yes, my boys got it right. How wise of them!

It is true, a good deep breath can work magic. It is soothing, it is pacifying. Deep breathing releases tense muscles and will calm the mind.

Practising some correct deep breathing exercises for just a few minutes, a few times a day, is sufficient to change the quality of our lives and improve our health.

This can be done anytime, anywhere. You do not need anyone to teach you, and it's available to you free of charge... how much easier can it be? You can practise while relaxing, or sitting at the desk, or while exercising, walking, or meditating.

BREATHING TO SUPPORT THE POSTURE AND TO FACILITATE MOVEMENT

Breathing exercises are very effective not only for reducing stress in the body and the mind but also for creating the proper muscle core connection and facilitating proper alignment to support our posture, in particular in our neck and shoulders. This will help us to maintain a more aligned posture while sitting for long hours at a desk or in front of a screen.

Breathing is also the link between the body and the mind. It is essential in the practice of meditation and it is the foundation of body-mind techniques such as yoga, tai chi, chi gong, martial arts, Pilates, Gyrotonic®, and other intelligent movement techniques.

Thousands of years ago, in India, the yogis had understood the importance of breathing as a tool to achieve a healthy body and a peaceful mind. They practised the art of breath control, "pranayama". The word "prana" means breath, and "ayama" means control.

Unfortunately, some of the information given today regarding breathing techniques is not correct, and this is causing some confusion. So often my clients have expressed that confusion and asked me: "My yoga teacher told me to breathe with my tummy, then I went to a Pilates class and they told me to do the opposite. I am so confused. How should I breathe?"

What exactly is correct breathing?

Today, we are presented with such a wide variety of different breathing techniques or breathing meditation techniques. There is way too much information and very often contradictory information. Different meditation techniques, yoga styles, martial arts, Pilates, and other exercise methods all require a particular breathing technique. All these methods certainly offer very valuable teachings and practices on how to improve our body-mind connection and how to achieve fluid and precise movements. But... first of all, before we start learning more advanced breathing techniques that will bring us to another level of movement connection or spiritual enlightenment, let's keep our feet firmly on the earth and practise breathing the way we were born to breathe.

HOW TO BREATHE CORRECTLY

It is very simple. **There is only one correct way to breathe**; we breathe using our lungs and our diaphragm muscles.

Diaphragmatic Breathing

Learning proper diaphragmatic breathing is the foundation for learning more advanced and more vigorous breathing techniques. Sadly, in our stressful and busy lifestyle, we have forgotten how to breathe efficiently. We have lost that full lung capacity of our ancestors, the full lung capacity of a mover and a runner.

Due to the long hours spent sitting hunched in front of a computer, driving, commuting and sitting in public transport, often in incorrect postural alignment, our contemporary generation is succumbing to the effects of a more sedentary and unhealthier lifestyle. We are gradually losing that natural connection, that innate lung capacity.

We are becoming more and more "accessory" or "shallow" breathers. This incorrect breathing is one of the main causes of the tension in our body and it is very often the root of the "pain in the neck" that plagues our generation.

Diaphragmatic breathing is the correct way of breathing, and the most efficient when moving and exercising. This correct breathing will create the right connection with our core muscles, and it will stabilise our spine during motion. As I have said in Chapter 3 in the Ferrari analogy, breathing is the key that will initiate your vehicle.

The diaphragm is the most efficient muscle during the process of breathing.

The diaphragm is a large muscle that is located horizontally across the base of the ribcage. It is connected in the front, along the sides of your lower ribs, and also along the back.

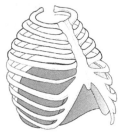

The key to mastering the art of breathing is to actively engage the diaphragm to serve as a pump to drive the breath in and out of the lungs.

Understanding diaphragmatic breathing

Find a comfortable place to sit and try to maintain your back as straight as you can. Place both feet on the ground, put your hands on your lap and let's begin!

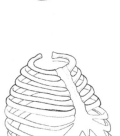

Take a deep breath in through your nose. **As you inhale**, the diaphragm muscle will descend towards the abdomen to facilitate the expansion of the lungs and allowing them to fill with air. This will create a lateral expansion of the thoracic cage.

As you exhale out of your mouth, the diaphragm will release and rise upward, allowing the lungs to expel the air, and the thoracic cage to tighten towards your waistline.

The neck and shoulders should not be used and raised; in diaphragmatic breathing you should concentrate on feeling as much as you can the action of the ribcage expanding and narrowing, just like the accordion musical instrument.

INCORRECT BREATHING

It is unfortunate that today some forms of exercises are often taught without the correct breathing instructions. Correct breathing is the main movement facilitator.

Some people believe that correct breathing happens when we force or balloon the abdomen, activating and exerting the abdominal muscles. Or they do not pay enough attention to a shallow pattern of breathing, which is when we focus only on the upper thoracic area, chest and clavicles (the collarbones).

Both belly breathing and shallow chest breathing are NOT THE CORRECT WAY TO BREATHE.

It would be very beneficial if exercise instructors, along with therapists, physicians and other professionals related to health and movement would teach what correct diaphragmatic breathing is. Teaching the correct way of breathing would help many people to improve their health, the quality of their life, and help them to better manage their stress.

BREATHING ACTIONS TO AVOID

Shallow or accessory chest breathing

This happens when we breathe using only the very upper part of the chest, the neck and shoulders.

As we inhale, we wrongly lift the collarbones and the shoulder, creating a lot of tension in the muscles around the neck the shoulder and the jaw area. This breathing is very inefficient and causes a lot of tension in the neck and shoulder muscles. Unfortunately, due to our sedentary lifestyle and the hours spent sitting in front of a computer this way of breathing is becoming very common.

Abdominal breathing

This happens when we, incorrectly, mainly involve our abdominal muscles and the belly during the breathing process. Many people expand the abdominal area too much when they breathe. They force the abdominal muscles outwards during the process of breathing, bloating their tummy like a balloon. This is also a very inefficient way of breathing. It will destabilize the core muscles and therefore the spine. It will create pelvic instability and compromise proper pelvic alignment and therefore our posture… and, aesthetically… who wants to see a protruding belly?

One of the most common comments I hear when I do my postural assessment is "I don't know how to breathe properly", or "I'm so confused, how am I supposed to breathe? Do I breathe with my stomach?" The stomach!!? I always answer the same way; God gave us a pair of lungs to breathe and a stomach to digest. Why would we breathe using the stomach?

When we are in the womb we breathe through our umbilical cord. When we are born our first action outside our mother's womb is that big gasp of air called LIFE. This is the first time we use our lungs, and we continue to do so for the rest of our lives. But if we observe babies, we see that they still tend to breathe with their tummies. As adults, we also breathe with our tummy when we sleep or when we enter into deep relaxation or meditative state, but when we are in movement and moving actively, proper diaphragmatic breathing is necessary to stabilize our core and facilitate movement.

So next time you are out in nature for a walk, pause for a moment and think how wonderful is to take that deep and refreshing breath into your lungs. After all, it's the first and last act of our life, so let's enjoy it to the FULL… take a deep breath and be thankful!

UNDERSTANDING YOUR OWN BREATHING PATTERN

For each of the following breathing exercises, taking a deep breath means **inhaling through the nose,** consciously filling the lungs with air from the lower to the upper part. The inhalation has to be done gently, without forcing it, and slowly counting 1… 2… 3…

Releasing a breath means exhaling **through the mouth**, funnelling that breath from your lungs starting from the top and allowing your ribcage to fall all the way towards your waist and hips. Again, slowly counting 1... 2... 3...

It can help to make a deep ahhhhhh sound as you exhale; this will facilitate your exhalation and the activation of the diaphragm muscle.

BREATHING EXERCISE
WITH A TOWEL

This is an easy and very effective breathing exercise that will teach you how to activate your core muscles, in particular, your diaphragm and your torso muscles.

Practise it every day for a couple of minutes standing or sitting in front of a mirror.

- Place a scarf or a long, thin towel around your thoracic cage.

- The towel will cross like an X where your diaphragm muscle is, on your solar plexus.

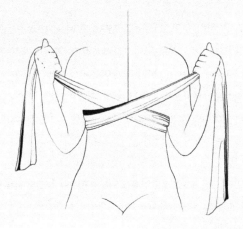

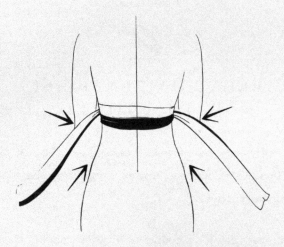

In order to avoid tension on your neck and shoulders, imagine you are placing a glass of your favourite drink on top of each shoulder. I personally like to imagine my favourite, a glass of champagne... you may be surprised to see how much tension you can create in your neck and shoulders after a few breaths, and how difficult it is to keep those imaginary glasses of champagne on your shoulders still.

As you slowly inhale through your **nose** and slowly exhale through your open **mouth,** observe the movement of your thoracic cage. Pay attention to how the neck and shoulders react to your breathing pattern. Most likely you will breathe by lifting the shoulders up and down (accessory breathing) instead of breathing from your diaphragm and abdominal muscles.

The focus should be **only where your towel is wrapped,** around your thoracic cage, and where the towel crosses in front of your diaphragm muscle.

Please, don't rush your breath. Slowly, count 1... 2... 3... as you inhale through your **nose,** and again 1... 2... 3... as you exhale through your **open mouth. As you practise your breathing, observe the sides of your thorax where the towel is wrapped.**

As you inhale, your thoracic cage should gently expand laterally, against the towel, which will create a slight resistance.

As you exhale, the thoracic cage should narrow, and the towel will tighten as it wraps around your diaphragm.

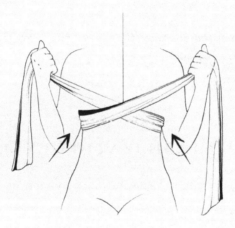

The towel should feel like a corset that loosens and tightens as you breathe in and out. You can also imagine your thoracic cage like an accordion, the musical instrument, which will expand laterally on the inhale and narrow on the exhale.

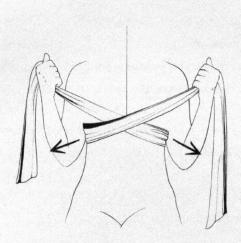

This activation of your thoracic muscles will finally create the perfect initiation to connect efficiently to your engine, the core. Now that your engine is on, you are ready to move.

BREATHING STABILIZATION EXERCISE

This breathing exercise will activate your core muscles. It is also a very powerful breathing exercise to give good breathing awareness. Practise this exercise for a few minutes when you wake each morning, before going to sleep, or while you are relaxing. It is also the perfect preparation **before starting any exercise routine.** When I teach my classes I always start with this breathing exercise to relax the person and create the right connection.

Breathing will initiate the connection between the muscles and the movement; remember, breathing is the KEY to start your engine. Correct breathing will connect you to the right movement.

When breathing, always inhale through your NOSE for steady counts of

1... 2... 3... and always exhale through your MOUTH for a steady count of 1... 2... 3... Keep your mouth slightly open and relaxed, and if you want to, make a nice sound, "haaaaa", as you exhale.

Lie comfortably on your back. Place a small pillow under your head, and bend your knees, placing both feet on the mat. Alternatively, if you feel more comfortable, place a big pillow under your knees to support your legs.

Scan your body from head to toe, and make sure you are very relaxed. Pay particular attention to the tension in your neck and shoulders. Relax and gently slide your shoulders and shoulder blades towards your waist away from your ears.

Turn your head side to side to make sure you don't have tension in your neck and open your mouth wide just like when you are yawning, to release any tension in the jaws.

Learn how to observe and become aware of your breathing pattern. You are now going to observe how your correct breathing creates the right connection with your core muscles. Starting from:

1. Focus on Chest

Place your hand on your chest. As you gently inhale through your nose and gently exhale through your mouth make sure that your shoulders do not rise up towards your ears. Your chest should naturally rise as you inhale, then gently move down and soften during the exhalation.

2. Focus on Ribcage

Place both hands on your ribcage. Continue with the same breathing pattern, inhale through your nose and gently exhale through your mouth, filling the lungs with air from the bottom up as you inhale, and emptying them from top to bottom as you exhale.

The ribcage should gently expand sideways as you inhale, narrow and gently slide down towards your waist as you exhale. The narrowing of the ribcage should feel as if you are tightening a corset as you exhale. Just like the towel exercise, or an accordion that expands and narrows as you are playing.

You can also visualise your lungs like some dry, thirsty sponges, and your breath as fresh water. As you inhale, the water reaches the dried sponges; from the bottom up, the sponges/lungs will swell with water. As you exhale, imagine gently squeezing the water out of the sponges from the top down, showering towards your abdomen, down towards your hips, glutes (the large muscles in your bottom) and pubic bones.

3. Focus on Abdomen

Now place your hands on your abdomen and, while you keep practising the previous thoracic breathing, focus on the abdomen area, and on your belly button (navel).

As you inhale, your abdomen should remain quite still and not bloat like a balloon; your inhalation has to fill your lungs.

As you exhale, funnelling your breath down towards your hips, you should feel a clear sensation of your abdominal muscles tightening **inwards** and **not pushing against your hands**. You should experience a feeling of tightening a corset or zipping up a pair of tight jeans.

Try again and now focus on your **belly button.** As you exhale, your belly button should sink deeper and deeper as if it wants to reach the spine. This will naturally draw the abdominal wall inwards. This is called NAVEL to SPINE breathing.

Finally, place your hands on top of your hip bones. Inhale and exhale, maintaining an awareness of your breathing, relax your neck and shoulders, feel your thorax expanding and narrowing like an accordion, feel your navel reaching to the spine and facilitating the drawing of the abdominal muscles inward. You should now experience a clear feeling of tightening the corset all the way from your upper abdomen through your waist and down to your pelvic area.

Note that during this breathing exercise the hips should remain still and relaxed. Especially as we try to tighten the abdominal muscles during the exhalation, we often tend to overuse the hip flexors and curl up the hips.

Practise this breathing stabilization exercise every day. You will feel the difference immediately.

NEUTRAL SPINE

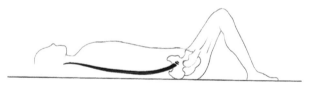

POSTERIOR PELVIC TILT

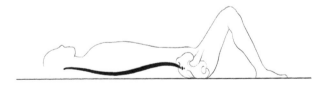

ANTERIOR PELVIC TILT

CHAPTER 7

POSTURE
Perfect

THE IMPORTANCE OF GOOD POSTURE

Postural alignment is the key to a strong, healthy, and fully efficient body.

Poise and good posture are the marks of a healthy, well-balanced body. Mentally, we may still stand and move with the grace of our youth, however, insidiously, without our consciously noticing, our poise may have softened; our posture melted a little or completely dissolved away. A lifestyle that has required a significant amount of time sitting will have taken its toll. Our posture, and consequently our spine, will have suffered.

In order to maintain a healthy body, we should encourage it to move the way it was designed to move. We can keep our bodies in alignment and operating at optimum efficiency. Unfortunately, we do not. In our lifestyle, the long hours sitting at a desk, or in a car, and the lack of exercise are factors that conspire to bend our body out of alignment. And for those who do lead an active life, not all types of activities promote proper alignment or good posture. Finally, not all physical activities are suitable for all people.

Good posture is the result of an efficient body; a body that moves intelligently in movement.

Though modern technology can help us with anti-ageing products; beauty products can help our skin appear younger and radiant, and plastic surgery can erase a few years from our face and parts of our body, nothing can beat the appearance of a strong, fit body and the confidence that that body exudes. That is the real secret of youthfulness!

No beauty products or surgery can help us to maintain an efficient body. It is simply a lifestyle choice and it requires a true commitment.

I believe that everyone can be that person exuding confidence and youth at any age. We simply have to move, develop better postural awareness and make the right choices for our body and our fitness programmes.

As I said at the beginning of my book, to maintain a youthful appearance and good POSTURE for the rest of your life, you need to keep your body in MOVEMENT.

So how do we keep a good posture? Or how do we get a good posture to keep? Or, even more important, what is GOOD POSTURE?

The technical definition of posture is:

The way we hold our body while standing, sitting or lying down. Good posture involves training our body to stand, walk, sit and lie in positions  where the least strain is placed on supporting muscles and ligaments during movement or weight-bearing activities.

The word "posture" comes from the Latin verb "ponere" which means "to put or to place".

There are many benefits when maintaining a GOOD POSTURE:

- *Prevents backache and muscular pain.*

- *Prevents the spine from being in abnormal positions.*

- *Prevents fatigue because muscles are being used more efficiently.*

- *Helps decrease the wearing of joint surfaces that could result in arthritis.*

- *Contributes to a good appearance.*

- *Will give you poise and confidence.*

How many times, when we were children, did we hear our parents or our teacher say, "Don't slouch!", "Sit up straight!", "Stand tall!", "Straighten up!", "Shoulders back!", "Straighten those shoulders!"? Although we, as children, may have heard these instructions many times, we didn't really understand what they meant. When teachers and parents gave these instructions, they were most likely quoting their own parents rather than understanding the technicalities of good posture.

As we grow more mature, we begin to realize that bad habits, lifestyle choices, injuries, or congenital/structural problems, all affect our efforts to achieve POSTURE PERFECTION.

Technically, the key for good posture is a HEALTHY SPINE, and the key to a healthy spine is good CORE SUPPORT. These two conditions go hand in hand, each dependent on the other!

Like the song 'Ebony and Ivory'

Think Spine and Core instead and sing the song in your head...

Healthy Spine and Core Support

Get together in perfect harmony...

Before I talk about some simple anatomical technicalities, I must draw your attention to the main purpose of this book. It is not to give you a list of exercises to fix your posture. I don't believe in exercising with a book in hand. Exercise is an activity that should be done with the guidance of appropriate professionals.

My purpose is to stimulate your interest in your body and guide you through the process of discovery and self-awareness. Trust me, once you have developed a postural awareness, you will have found your PERFECT POSTURE for the rest of your life.

How many times have I heard in my practice the same comment, "My posture is terrible; I wish I could do something to fix it!"

The 3 steps FOR FIXING a problem are:

1. *To be aware of it*

2. *To understand it*

3. *To find the solution*

STEP 1: AWARENESS

Postural Imbalances

Postural problems and imbalances come mainly from two sources:

Congenital/Structural

This is when we are born with a structural misalignment, which is very often genetic. Examples: spine scoliosis, spine kyphosis (hunched spine), knock knees, flat feet and others.

Lifestyle/Bad Habits

During my assessment, I look at what may have caused the body to lose its proper postural Alignment.

The most common causes are:

1.   *Sedentary lifestyle*

2.   *Weak core muscles*

3.   *Lack of body awareness*

4.   *Sitting at a desk or computer for long hours*

5.   *An injury*

6.   *Operation; post-rehabilitation*

7.   *Pregnancies*

8.   *Even the way we carry our school bag, briefcase, groceries, or children can affect our posture*

9.   *Unsuitable exercise regime*

This list is by no means finite. These are the most common causes.

All these aspects of our daily life are very important factors which determine the way we carry ourselves and, eventually, affect our postural alignment.

It is my personal opinion that it does not matter if the cause is congenital, the result of bad habits, or a medical condition. What matters to me is that your body is suffering an imbalance, and we need to take care of it. We cannot change the structure and alignment of our bones (unless we are forced to take the extreme action of an orthopaedic operation,) but we can certainly change the muscles and their movement patterns by strengthening them or relieving the tension. Strong and yet flexible muscles will create the right support for your posture. And it is NEVER too late. This can be done at ANY TIME, at ANY AGE.

STEP 2: UNDERSTANDING

To have a better understanding of our postural alignment it is necessary to first look at and to understand our spine.

A healthy spine has natural curves.

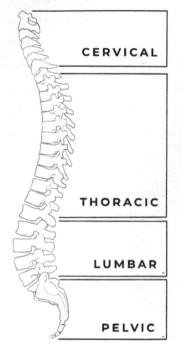

CERVICAL

THORACIC

LUMBAR

PELVIC

• *The neck, or the cervical spine, curves slightly inward.*

• *The mid-back, or thoracic spine, is curved outward.*

• *The lower back, or the lumbar spine, curves inward again.*

• *Pelvic spine, tailbone curves slightly inward.*

Neutral Spine

When we think of good posture, we immediately think of pulling our shoulders back and contracting our abdominals; this is incorrect.

In a clinical environment and intelligent movement, the concept of good spine alignment is referred to as "neutral spine". Neutral spine is the position in which your neck, back and pelvis are correctly placed under the least amount of stress and strain. This allows the spine to function correctly without damage and, therefore, without pain.

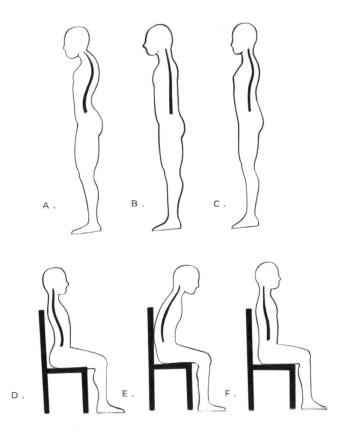

A. TOO ARCHED   B. TOO FLATTENED   C. NEUTRAL (GOOD POSTURE)
D. TOO ARCHED   E. SLOUCHING   F. NEUTRAL (GOOD POSTURE)

Neutral alignment is important in helping to cushion the spine from excessive stress and strain. It will allow the shock absorbers of our vehicle to work at optimum efficiency.

I compared at the beginning of the book the neutral spine to the neutral gear, the parking gear of our beautiful vehicle: the starting point from which we move our vehicle.

Understanding the neutral spine position is the key to keeping a GOOD and EFFICIENT POSTURE as well as preventing back pain and back injuries.

Ideally, a neutral spine should be maintained while sitting, standing, walking, and performing any physical activity.

I believe that maintaining a neutral spine is the key to an efficient, healthy, balanced body, while a non-neutral spine leads to "improper posture" and puts increased stress on your back, causing discomfort – and it may even lead to injury.

These concepts are at the base of intelligent movement techniques.

A non-neutral spine, poor posture, can develop as a result of:

- *A sedentary lifestyle*

- *Lack of posture awareness*

- *Weak core muscles*

- *An injury*

- *A person's congenital/structural problem*

If you are following any exercise programme your instructor must make sure that you are performing these exercises in a proper postural alignment. If not, most probably you will not get the right results or even worse you will risk being injured.

Remember that you will be driving your beautiful car out of alignment and inefficiently, with no results and with energy waste.

Common spine pathologies: Scoliosis, kyphosis and lordosis

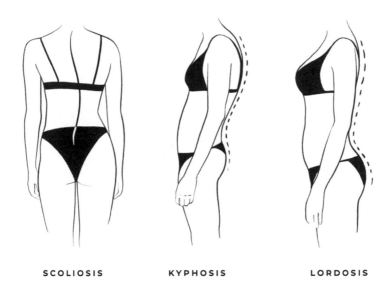

SCOLIOSIS   KYPHOSIS   LORDOSIS

SCOLIOSIS is a lateral curvature of the spine, either in the upper (thoracic) or lower (lumbar) area, or, in a worst-case scenario, both. The spine will look like the letter S.

People who have scoliosis develop a very pronounced postural imbalance that will eventually, affect the entire body alignment and movement functionality.

Even a small curve of the spine can cause an imbalance that can be reflected in your hips, your gearbox. This will limit your vehicle's ability to run smoothly and efficiently. It is congenital.

KYPHOSIS is the increased curvature of the upper spine. It can be congenital or caused by lifestyle choices. It is very common with people sitting long hours at a desk or computer and lack of proper core muscles support.

LORDOSIS is an increased curvature of the lower spine. It, too, can be congenital or caused by lifestyle choices. It is very common among people who have weak pelvic floor muscles, and pregnant women. It is also common among dancers and gymnasts, due to the overextension of muscles during their exercise routines.

Other parts of the body where misalignment can affect your posture are:

KNEES

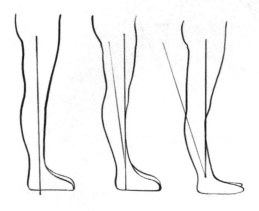

1. NEUTRAL   2. OVEREXTENDED

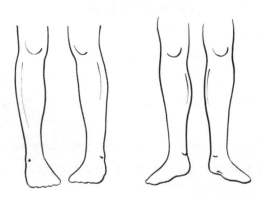

3. INTERNALLY & EXTERNALLY ROTATED KNEES

LEGS

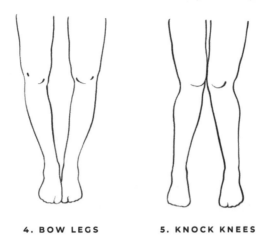

4. BOW LEGS   **5. KNOCK KNEES**

FEET

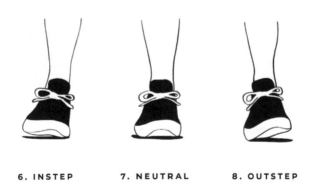

6. INSTEP   **7. NEUTRAL**   **8. OUTSTEP**

All of these aspects of structural misalignments are very important factors which determine the way you carry yourself.

If you want to have a better understanding of your posture, tactfully observe your parents or siblings. It is always easier to see in others what you cannot see in yourself. If you notice any misalignment, it is likely to be a genetic condition, passing down through the generations. **But the safest way** to have your POSTURE assessed is by a professional.

It is no bad thing to know of a personal misalignment, and it is not the end of the world... rather, it is the beginning of a better, pain-free, more comfortable and healthier life in movement.

Look at me, for example, I have a very mild congenital scoliosis in my lower back which was undiagnosed for many years. This has been the root of all of my back problems since I was young. As a dancer, I had to adapt my mildly curved spine to very challenging dance moves. Since our body is such an amazing, intelligent and adaptable vehicle, my muscles adapted to compensate for that misalignment, creating an imbalance invisible to the untrained eye. Truly it looked good when I danced and lifted my legs, but it did not feel good, especially as I grew older! Eventually, that misalignment resulted in me suffering a severe back injury and, thereafter, severe chronic back pain.

The muscles that become involved in the compensation of a misalignment are not necessarily the right ones, and this is too often the source of most chronic injuries, as happened with me.

STEP 3: FINDING THE SOLUTION

How to improve our posture?

The one true answer to a good postural alignment is maintaining a correct spine position and in order to do so, we need to develop strong CORE support.

Remember the little song and sing it in your head:

"Healthy Spine and Core support

Get together in perfect harmony" – and to develop strong core support we need to move and exercise. There is no other recipe. I will develop this concept in more detail in Chapter 9, THE CORE ISSUE.

HOW DO WE ASSESS OUR POSTURE?

I am well aware that it is not easy to assess our own posture and I strongly advise you to seek the advice of a suitable professional; he/she will understand your postural imbalances and advice you on the most suitable programme to improve your posture.

Ivana Daniell BODY ID Postural and Movement Assessment

Over the years I have designed and refined a postural analysis and a posture correction programme that are suitable for everyone, from the desk-bound executive to the champion triathlete. My assessment recognises that each person's body is unique, and each person's choice of physical regime will be different.

The aim of my assessment is to ensure that informed and intelligent options are passed to you about how you can take care of your body, and how you can choose an appropriate exercise programme that will most benefit your body and improve your lifestyle.

The 90-minute assessment is suitable for those:

- *Embarking on a new fitness regime.*

- *Currently pursuing a fitness regime.*

- *With a recurring muscle or joint pain, or with an injury*

- *Who want to be educated about postural awareness*

- *Searching for an alternative and more nurturing environment.*

- *Searching for a better quality of life through Intelligent Movement.*

My Postural Assessment is also suitable for anyone who wants a professional and objective assessment of their body's alignment, range of movement, and advice on how to get optimum results from an exercise regime. Many of us have experienced some level of neck, shoulder or back pain, which may be attributed to postural problems. My aim is to help people make the right choices, or if they are practising any sport or exercise, identify areas of their exercise regime that can be improved, in a safe and healthy way.

EXERCISE

Assess your own body

Although it is important that you seek an assessment by a professional, I want you to participate in your own assessment to gain more awareness of your posture.

I strongly advise you to share this experience with your partner, with a sibling or with a friend, someone you feel very comfortable with. You can observe each other's posture and make it a fun experience.

You need a full-length mirror and to wear either a swimsuit or some tight-fitting clothes.

Do not to cover your legs and be barefoot.

Use the body drawings on the next page to mark your notes and your findings.

Start by standing in front of the mirror with parallel feet, and take a minute or two to observe the following:

• Are you putting equal weight on both feet, both legs?

• Do you feel you are leaning more to the right or to the left?

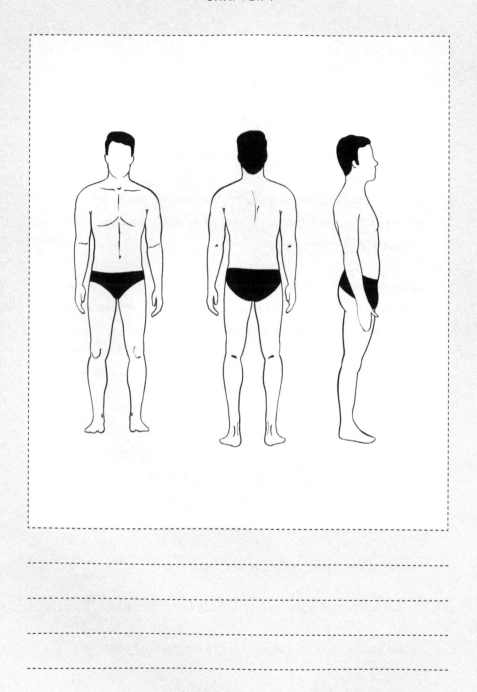

Observe the following:

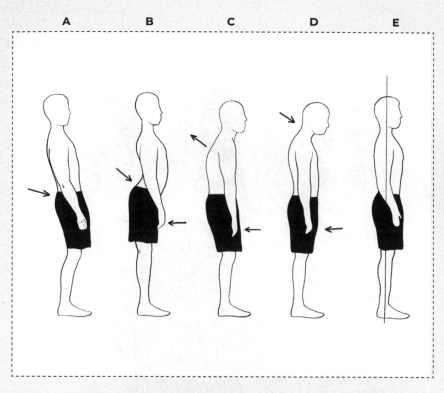

LOWER BACK

A. Is your back swaying backward? ....

B. Has it got an increased extension? ....

UPPER BACK

C. Has it got a pronounced curve?...

D. Are your shoulders slouching?...

HEAD, NECK

D. Your head and your chin; are they protruding forward causing an increased compression on your cervical spine? ....

E. Can you easily hold good neutral posture?....................................

Remember, it is important you share this experience with a partner; four eyes are always better than two. Do not be judgmental of your body and try your best to be a neutral observer. I advise the same to your partner, his/her observations have to be purely postural and never based on negative aesthetical judgment. Only by being detached from any self-judgment will you be able to achieve a better **awareness** and have a better **understanding and**, therefore, to get the most appropriate measures **to fix** your postural problems.

You have previously assessed your BODY TYPE and MOVEMENT PERSONALITY. Now you have assessed your POSTURE. I am sure you are starting to have a much clearer idea about your BODY ID.

CHAPTER 8

The COMPUTER GENERATION: *A pain in the neck*

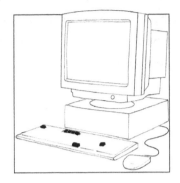

Computers, smartphones and modern technology are the active enemies of our posture.

Computers are increasingly replacing both professional and leisure activities. From business meetings and conference calls to online shopping and entertainment, we spend most of our day bound to a chair staring at a screen.

There can be nothing worse for a body that was designed to move for survival; a body that craves movement. Already we see the devastating effects of this sedentary lifestyle all around us. In my practice, I listen on a daily basis to people complaining of chronic neck, shoulder and back pain because they are desk-bound in front of a computer most of their day. Eventually, some of these chronic aches and pains could develop into more serious spine pathologies, which can be extremely painful and debilitating. There is no escape!

And those at even greater risk are our children. They are the future computer generation.

They will be the ones in the future who will pay the price of a virtual world and of a non-movement-orientated lifestyle, where more and more activities, from school and homework to fun and social activities, are done in front of a screen.

I wish to share here my personal experience as a parent.

My youngest son, Chris' passion since he was a very young child was nature, and in particular marine science. Living in a big city at 14 years old was quite a challenge, even though Singapore offered a lot of outdoor activities. Like most of his teenage friends, Chris' life was divided between school, back home doing homework, and spending some leisure time at the computer. We had to make a big decision. Chris wished to study in a school in the US that was very ecologically and nature-orientated. A perfect preparation for his future studies in marine science, his true passion. It was a tough decision for me as an Italian mama; the idea of separating from my son was akin to torture. However, the Holderness boarding school in New Hampshire, USA, along with a very strong academic curriculum, offered many leisure activities; among these were daily outdoor sports such as skiing, soccer, and various other sports. The school made a point that students would spend a fair amount of time daily practising outdoor sport and activities. Chris very happily joined the Holderness boarding school, located in the beautiful woods of New Hampshire. Because of a healthy and active outdoor lifestyle, he soon transformed into a handsome, fit and confident young man. By the time he left, he had grown tall and strong, and his posture was perfect. The power of movement! Today Chris is 27 and he is about to complete his Master's in Marine Science in the UK.

When I see city children dividing all their time between school at a desk and at home in front of a screen, I feel very sad.

I remember, with nostalgia, my healthy childhood in Sicily, where climbing the trees in our garden, going for a bike ride with friends, going to the beach or, in my particular case, dancing in a pink tutu were considered the most exciting forms of leisure.

It is a doomed future that our children are facing: a non-movement-orientated future lifestyle that will surely lead to a life plagued with chronic aches and pains and weight problems.

We need to be seriously aware of the damage that can result from living in this virtual world and start educating our children about the importance of movement and good posture. We need to be encouraging them to lead a healthier outdoor and movement-orientated lifestyle. This should be our mission as responsible parents.

My mission, my vision, goes even further. I dream of a new concept of School Physical Education, where children are properly educated from the beginning of their school life on how to understand their body and the dangers of a non-movement-orientated lifestyle, or the damage caused by long hours spent in front of computers and sitting at desks that do not support a healthy posture.

A school environment is an excellent place to provide the right guidance and an appropriate programme of postural education.

Over the years education departments have introduced classes on personal hygiene, personal grooming and sex education. Why not introduce the most important health issue of all, **posture and physical education**?

The biggest challenge would start with re-evaluating the configuration of the classrooms. The way our children are sitting at their school desks is totally unsuitable and schools should seriously consider a much more posture-friendly environment. After all, these children are our future!

In order to give a healthier environment to my son, I had to decide to send him to a school in the woods, and literally back to the roots. Not all children can be given this opportunity and not all parents may consider being separated from their children a viable option. Mine was a big sacrifice, but it was worth it!

When I lived in Singapore, I created special classes for teens. It was hard to convince 13- and 14-year-old teens to join a Pilates class and educate them about the importance of a good posture. With the help and support of my wonderful clients and intelligent parents, my teens' classes became a big success. I awakened the interest of these boys and girls and planted the seeds for their future postural development. It is wonderful to see how young people respond so well to a different and intelligent approach to exercise.

MY TIPS

How to keep a GOOD POSTURE
while working at your desk

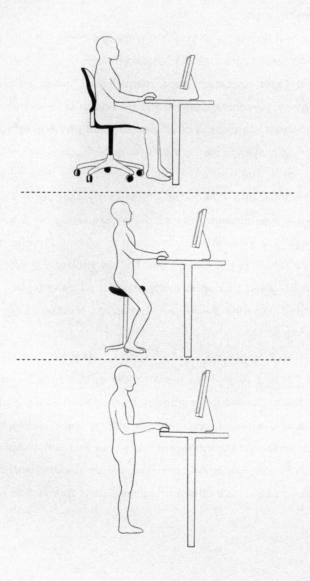

Sitting at your desk

Sit on a good chair, an ergonomic chair would be ideal. These chairs are specially designed to give you proper hip and back support during the long sitting hours.

The most important thing is the height of your chair; the lower the chair, the worse it is for your back. The best is to create a 120-degree angle at your hips (as you see in the picture below). Ergonomic chairs are adjustable to your preferred height.

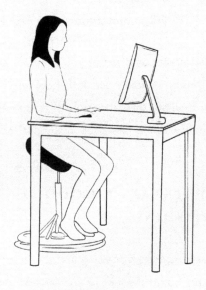

Keep legs uncrossed, and feet flat on the floor.

Sit with your body weight distributed equally on both hips. The fact that ergonomic chairs do not have a back-support is good, for two reasons:

1. You are not leaning back, so you are activating your core muscles to maintain your spine upright; I call this active sitting.

2. You will get tired and feel the need to get up for a few minutes for a coffee break. This will avoid slouching at your chair and maintaining an incorrect posture... and it's good to get a break from sitting and move your legs.

Your desk should be at a suitable height. To adjust it, you can buy a special tray that you can easily place on top of the desk and adjust it to your preferred height.

Position the monitor of your computer at eye level, and keep your shoulders relaxed. This will prevent stress on your neck and shoulder area.

Take a nice deep breath as often as you can; lack of proper breathing will create tension in your neck and shoulders. A proper breathing pattern will facilitate the relaxation of tense neck and shoulder muscles (See the breathing exercises in Chapter 6, The Importance of Breathing).

HOW TO MAINTAIN A GOOD POSTURE WHILE STANDING

Today some health experts are advising that you alternate sitting at your desk with standing, but this requires a special ergonomic desk that can be changed in height so that it is suitable for your standing position.

In my opinion this solution is good if you are very posture aware and maintain a good standing position while working at the desk. Standing incorrectly can put some stress on your lower back and result in pain.

The other challenge is that most people working in offices do not have a choice of workstation, they have to adapt to what is given, and often their sitting/working environment is not very posture supportive. Most of my clients have created their own workstation at their home. I have advised them to invest in a good ergonomic chair and they have created, under my guidance, their ideal workstation.

If you are considering standing at your desk, I advise the following:

While standing it is most important to maintain correct postural alignment, a neutral alignment. You should have an equal weight bearing on both legs and feet. Correct alignment allows your body to operate at its optimum and avoid muscular stress. Proper foot support is essential, so choose your footwear carefully. Ladies, when standing, avoid high heels.

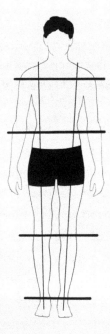 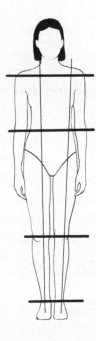

XAVIER'S STORY

A pain in the neck

Xavier's story is a perfect testimonial of what hours of sitting at the desk and working long hours at a computer can do to your posture and to your body.

When I met Xavier, I was living in Singapore. He was 35 years old. He was a mathematics schoolteacher and spent part of his day sitting at the desk while teaching, and the rest of his time still sitting at a desk correcting students' homework, working long hours on the computer.

His main complaint was chronic neck and shoulder pain that caused him frequent severe and debilitating headaches.

His posture was very poor, and his back was starting to show a prominent hunch.

Though Xavier was naturally blessed with a good body, tall and slim, and pleasantly good-looking, the quite sedentary life due to the nature of his job was starting to take its toll.

Xavier had tried going to the gym, but after a few sessions the pain in his neck and shoulders became unbearable, and his headaches even more frequent. His body objected strongly to this regime, and sadly he had to stop any form of exercise altogether. The famous "Catch 22" situation (See page 177).

During the postural assessment, I had a good look at Xavier. It was clear that though he was a naturally active person, slim and blessed with a good physique, years of sitting hunched over a desk marking or working on his PC for long hours, combined with a lack of appropriate exercise, were the cause of his "pain in the neck" and the deterioration of his posture.

His "pain in the neck" was quite visible. He had a protruded neck, chin forward and kyphotic (hunched) back. His neck and shoulders were extremely tense, and his neck and shoulder alignment greatly compromised. His body lacked general muscle tone due to the lack of movement and exercise during the past few years.

It was as though, in his own words, someone had pushed down hard on his head so that his neck felt as if it had been pushed into his shoulders. He could feel this constant tension and compression.

Clearly, I needed to choose a programme where I could help ease the pain and reorganize the muscles in the neck and shoulder area. This would free him from the constant tension and compression that was the cause of his ever-present pain and uncomfortable headaches.

After discussing in detail his lifestyle habits and his goals I created a suitable programme for Xavier.

The first exercises that I chose, simple breathing exercises, would release the tension from his neck and shoulders and alleviate his pain and headaches.

Then, in the second stage, I worked specifically on the neck and shoulder muscle organization, while strengthening the core muscles in order to better support the neck and shoulder area. It was important to improve both his postural alignment and his postural awareness, which had been compromised by years of bad habits.

First of all, I educated Xavier on how to sit at the desk and reviewed his work desk or workstation organization. He had spent all these hours slouching and tensing his shoulders. He needed to be more aware of the way he sat when working.

At the same time, we started our programme with a combination of exercises that helped him to develop strong core support and improve his postural alignment. We worked specifically on neck and shoulder organization. We then added Gyrotonic® exercises that helped him to improve his thoracic spine extension. The Gyrotonic® method also helped him to improve his stamina and movement coordination.

I also designed a simple 15-minute daily routine that he could practise at home.

It was hard at the beginning to convince a young man that "No pain, No gain" was no longer the way to go in order to get fit and feel better.

In intelligent movement he had to work differently. In order to make a transformation, Xavier had to understand the cause and the nature of his pain and be aware of its source. He had then, under my guidance, to find the right path and the right tools to make the transformation happen.

Xavier's body was also craving to be moved, to exercise. But we had to do it in the right way.

And we finally did it; it took us three full months. Xavier had an amazing quality; he was very diligent and took the programme extremely seriously. He attended three classes per week regularly at my centre in Singapore, never missing one. The more he noticed the changes, the more motivated he became.

After a few sessions with me, the headaches and "pain in the neck" were gone. After only a few weeks his neck and shoulders were looking much more relaxed, and the feeling of compression had disappeared.

After a few months, Xavier's body had changed. The visible hunch was gone. His shoulders were wide and strong, his neck long and relaxed. Xavier was now standing handsome and tall, proudly showing a well-defined and well-toned body.

Later Xavier asked me to teach him a series of suitable exercises that he could practise on his own at home or when he was away on holiday.

Xavier took the programme I gave him as his regular exercise regime. This time he worked under my motto "No Pain, Yes Gain". His look and his life had changed. He had become so disciplined that, when not at my studio, he would practise his exercise routines at home or at work on a daily basis.

Eventually, Xavier went back to his country of origin, South America. I spoke to Xavier recently. What a pleasure to hear that today, he feels strong and fit, and his life is no longer "a pain in the neck".

"I still practise regularly all the exercises that you taught me," he told me, *"and when I do go for an exercise class, I apply the movement principles that you taught me in your studio in Singapore. They are now imprinted in my body, in the muscles' memory; they will stay with me forever."*

CHAPTER 9

The **CORE** *Issue*

Who has not dreamed of a beautiful flat and well-defined tummy? Men and women, young or old, at any age, all want to look trim, taut and fit. The complaint I hear most from my friends and clients is, "Look at my tummy. It is so big, so flabby! I hate it! Before I had my children, I was so flat. Look at me now! Since I spend hours sitting at the desk I look like a blob!"

Even teenagers are body-conscious and self-conscious today. They want to expose a nice flat tummy or a six-pack at the beach or on social media; there is no doubt that a nice flat tummy looks good on everyone at any age. It is truly the secret of the svelte, youthful, and ageless look.

No matter what age a person is, a strong and well-defined core, along with a strong and well-balanced posture, will always make you stand out in a room, and will always make you look good, young and fit.

A strong core goes, as I have said in my little song, in perfect harmony with good posture. A good posture will free you of unwanted aches and pains; together they will enable you to live a healthy life in alignment, and in movement.

Building and maintaining a strong CORE support will enable you to finally escape that Catch 22 situation that inhibits most of our lives. We can all relate to it, that horrible vicious circle of "I am in pain and I can't move. I need to exercise to make the pain go away but I can't exercise till the pain goes away because it hurts too much."

It's a vicious circle! A Catch 22.

A strong core is the escape key from our Catch 22…

I was once the perfect example of that Catch 22 situation.

After my first child, Vinci, was born by Caesarean section, I returned to dancing far too soon and long before my body was ready for such rigorous exercise. I was in constant pain, and I wrongly thought that if I exercised harder it would go away.

My pelvic and abdominal muscles had not had a chance to recover the stress of both a pregnancy and an operation. They were extremely weak. My body was totally out of alignment. My lumbar (lower back) vertebrae could not take that stress as they were lacking the support of a good core and pelvic floor support, so they finally gave in.

It took me years to recover from that injury, and guess what? Although I tried many recommended remedies, only one thing worked. I HAD to rebuild a very strong core support. As a bonus, my tummy looked just perfect, nice and flat. Even today, people still do not understand that one of the secrets of my youthful looks is my wonderful, strong natural corset.

When I do my postural assessment and see my clients for the first time, I require them to complete a questionnaire. One of the questions I ask is what they would like to achieve out of the programme, and 80% answer that they wish to achieve a STRONG CORE.

Although many today are aware there is a "CORE ISSUE", we need to understand how to achieve a strong core.

THE MYTH OF THE ABDOMINALS

I have observed that many people don't really know what core muscles are, or how to exercise them properly.

Most people think that the core muscles are only the front abdominals, the six-pack. This is not correct. In truth, frontal abdominal muscles have a very limited action.

Some also believe that having strong six-pack abdominals is the foundation for good core strength. This also is incorrect. The abdominal muscles are only a small part of what makes up the core, our engine.

Many people are not aware of what and where the core muscles are, they also believe they have been doing the right abdominal exercises at a gym. They keep saying "Oh yes, I do my crunches every day," or "Yes, I do a lot of abdominals exercises". They don't understand, or I should perhaps say they have not been properly informed, that the famous crunches will not help them to develop proper core strength. They have not been properly instructed on how to exercise and strengthen their core muscles or told where exactly these muscles are and how to activate them.

Our search is not a lost cause; we can change our body, strengthen any muscle, improve our strength, our postural alignment, and rebuild a strong core at any time or at any age. We just have to do it the right way, in an intelligent way, choosing the right programme for our specific body and needs and, most of all, with the guidance of the right professional.

Do you remember at the beginning of the book when I described to you the perfect vehicle, the beautiful Ferrari we are born with? What makes that Ferrari run and roar is its perfectly engineered powerful engine.

In our body that engine is our core. Without it the vehicle will not run.

A strong core is the powerful engine of our vehicle that will facilitate any movement.

THE CORE MUSCLES, THE GIRDLE, THE CORSET

 I always give my clients the image of the core muscles as a girdle, or one of those old-fashioned corsets that women used to wear. The corset had to be strong but at the same time flexible. In the old times fabric was strengthened with whalebone stays, slim rods that held the body in position while laced tightly into an hourglass shape. How ecologically incorrect!

When I was a child in the 60s, my beautiful and perfectly poised grand-mother Memi used to tell me that women did not look the same as they used to. She showed me beautiful pictures from when she was young, commenting on how women used to carry themselves with such elegance, grace and poise. They were all corseted. They could hardly breathe or eat, but they certainly looked elegant. But at what cost! I used to ask my Memi, why did they have to be all laced up, when they could just keep it naturally? I was a ballerina, and also a child of the bra liberation generation. Corsets were out of the question!

But my grandmother was right. Keeping that beautiful poise and not having a big tummy sticking out was certainly the right way to carry oneself with elegance and grace. She was the living proof of it. She had also chosen a more practical and corset-free life. She looked amazing until the end of her life. Her figure was just perfect. Even my friends commented on her fit figure and flat tummy and on how young she looked even in her late 70s. One thing my Memi was doing right; she was a very active and sporty person. She was always in movement. When she took us to the mountains for long walks, her favourite activity, she was always the first to arrive at our destination, followed by the exhausted panting family, including us children. I was very fortunate, as my grandmother not only brainwashed me about always being elegantly poised, but also taught me to live a very active and movement-orientated lifestyle. Also, my years of ballet highlighted the importance of keeping good and strong CORE muscles.

UNDERSTANDING THE ROLE OF THE CORE MUSCLES

In movement everything comes from the CORE. If you don't have strong core muscles, you will not be able to move functionally. A gymnast or dancer who hasn't developed a strong core will not be able to leap in the air and still look feather light. For athletes, a strong CORE is one of the main keys to achieving maximum performance. For everyone else, a strong core is the secret to a pain-free, healthy back.

In intelligent movement core strength is what keeps your body in good alignment and optimum functionality.

Joseph Pilates wrote about the importance of core strength in *Return to Life through Contrology* (1928). He had based his new methodology on the importance of muscle control, creating a body-mind connection. His new method focused on the core postural muscles and the importance of the core strength. He was a pioneer and changed the way we exercise today.

The CORE actually consists of many different muscles that run along the entire length of the torso, front and back, including inner thigh, hamstrings, glutes and pelvic floor. They create a natural corset that supports our posture.

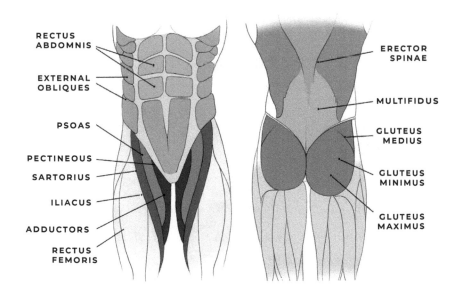

RECTUS ABDOMNIS

EXTERNAL OBLIQUES

PSOAS

PECTINEOUS

SARTORIUS

ILIACUS

ADDUCTORS

RECTUS FEMORIS

ERECTOR SPINAE

MULTIFIDUS

GLUTEUS MEDIUS

GLUTEUS MINIMUS

GLUTEUS MAXIMUS

The main role of these muscles is to stabilize the spine, the pelvis and the shoulders. They also help to maintain a neutral spine and therefore a healthy and functional posture.

The core muscles are the ones that ensure we stand upright, have good balance, and allow us to freely move our arms and legs. Without their support we would not be able to walk, and our body would not work efficiently.

These muscles also help us to control our movements, and to shift our body weight in different directions.

The core muscles are the foundation of our movements and posture.

Most neck and back problems are related to a weak core. Strong, balanced core muscles will help maintain appropriate posture and reduce strain on the spine.

Training the core muscles also corrects postural imbalances that can lead to injuries. The biggest benefit of strengthening the core muscles is to develop functional fitness – meaning fitness that will improve how we experience our daily activities.

BENEFITS OF A STRONG CORE

A strong core will:

- *Give you a strong and healthy posture and stability to support an efficient gait.*

- *Maintain you in proper alignment and free you from pain.*

- *Help you in the rehabilitation of back injuries.*

- *Support you with jobs that involve physical efforts such as lifting, or standing for long hours.*

- *Support you while practising your favourite sport or exercise programme and maximize your performance.*

- *Support you with jobs that require long sitting hours at the desk.*

- *Support you in your basic everyday activities.*

- *Give you a more youthful appearance.*

- *And, as a BONUS, you will look good and feel confident.*

THE IMPORTANCE OF PELVIC STABILITY, THE FOUNDATION AND ANCHOR OF OUR CORE

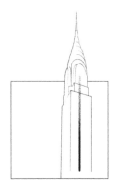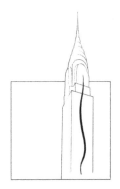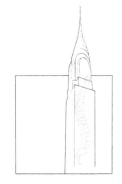

When I think of our torso I also like to think like an architect. I think of the torso as a beautiful building or perfectly engineered skyscraper. If the building is collapsing, or is starting to show structural problems, where do I look first? Certainly, I don't start up in the penthouse or at the 20th floor. I go straight to the foundations of the building. That is the first thing which needs to be checked and corrected. Only when the foundation is solid and stable can the rest of the structure be solid and perfect. Then I work my way up.

Pelvic stability is the foundation of our posture to achieve a strong core. It is the foundation of that perfectly engineered building or skyscraper.

Learning to properly recruit the deep stabilizer and the pelvic floor muscles is the key to a strong, stable core, a healthy spine and a good posture.

THE PELVIC FLOOR MUSCLES

The pelvic floor is made up of layers of muscles and other connective tissue. These layers stretch like a hammock from the tailbone at the back to the pubic bone in front. They support the reproductive organs and the bladder.

The pelvic floor muscles are important for bladder and bowel control. They also support healthy sexual functioning. It is vital to keep these muscles strong. The pelvic floor is the main support structure for the pelvic organs.

And yes... both men and women have pelvic floor muscles. How often have I heard people say in surprise, "Do men have a pelvic floor? I thought only women had a pelvic floor?" Anatomically both genders have pelvic floor muscles, although there is a difference.

In men such muscles are generally more stable. Simply, men don't carry babies and do not have such large hormonal fluctuations as women do.

Nevertheless, in men, these muscles can also become weakened. The main causes would be a prostate operation, urinary problems, chronic constipation, being overweight, a lumbar spine pathology or an abdominal operation.

In women these muscles tend to be much weaker as they are affected by hormonal fluctuations, pregnancies, the process of giving birth and, later, by the hormonal changes of menopause. As they are related to so many changes and challenges, these muscles are easily weakened and can become very unstable, causing problems such as bladder incontinence and prolapsed uterus.

I will talk in more depth about the female pelvic floor in Chapter 10, WOMEN'S HEALTH.

BEST EXERCISE PROGRAMMES TO IMPROVE CORE STRENGTH

All exercise activities performed correctly will require a CORE activation.

The Pilates Method focuses most of its methodology on core awareness and strengthening.

Specific core programmes are available online, hundreds and hundreds of them; please be aware most of them are harmful to a non-professional or elite mover.

Creating a healthy breathing pattern is the foundation for a healthy and strong CORE. You have quite a few breathing exercises in my manual to give you a good foundation. Think of those breathing exercises as the electrical initiation of your vehicle to start the engine, your CORE.

Start with the breathing stabilization exercise, on page 130

I have created some effective programmes for strengthening your core muscles efficiently and without risk of injuries.

Check my website **www.ivanadaniell.com**

CAN WE IMPROVE OUR CORE MUSCLES ONLY BY WALKING?

Walking is the most functional form of exercise, and it's free. It is very beneficial to both your posture and your core strength. You should make it a regular habit to walk for at least 30 to 45 minutes a day.

It would be ideal if you can complement it with an appropriate core exercise programme, twice a week. This would optimise your expected results.

Keep your posture in correct alignment and practise correct breathing while walking, and you can improve the activation of the core muscles and therefore increase their strength.

EXERCISE WITH AN APPLE

A simple apple or an unbreakable round object can be the perfect tool to practise this exercise and to feel if we use the abdominal muscles correctly. You will need to lie down on your back for this exercise.

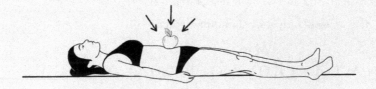

Place your apple on top of your belly button.

While you practise the breathing exercise you have learned in the breathing chapter, navel to spine breathing, see if you can keep the apple steady on top of your navel, or even better if can hold it deeper and deeper, as if you are nesting it.

Your abdominal muscles should not exert, or balloon and push the apple out; they should instead relax inward, and you should feel the sensation of the navel dropping deeper and deeper towards the spine. I call it nesting; imagine you are creating a concave space where the apple wants to settle and remains still and zip deeper down to hold the apple steady.

Note that during this breathing exercise the hips should remain still and in a neutral position. Especially as we try to tighten the abdominal muscles during the exhalation, we often tend to overuse the hip flexors and curl up the hips.

Also keep shoulders relaxed and try to avoid short, shallow breathing.

WOMEN'S HEALTH
Pregnancy & Menopause

When explaining to women the postural changes that occur during pregnancy, it is my mission to inform them about the amazing changes and challenges that pregnancy and motherhood will bring to their bodies, to their posture and eventually to their appearance.

Many mums-to-be will get so taken up and busy with the planning of their baby's growth and arrival that they often disregard the changes to their physique and to their posture. They carry on with their lives, their jobs, until one day they wake up with excruciating lower back pain, and they don't know what to do. Sadly, they will accept the pain as a part of the pregnancy package, carrying on until delivery, and in a worst-case scenario, accepting the injury way after the baby is born until it has become a chronic problem.

We can easily avoid this common scenario. If we are well prepared, we can enjoy an easy pregnancy, a speedy recovery and quickly regain a good figure.

The first thing I do with my client mums-to-be is to educate them about the changes and the challenges that their bodies will have to bear during these nine months. I will also teach them how to prevent any risk of back problems developing during the pregnancy and, after delivery, developing a strong and healthy core and a good postural alignment.

In order to avoid some of the inconveniences of pregnancy it is essential for us women to understand these natural changes, to be in touch with our body and accept these changes as a gift of life.

A mother needs to be strong, to face not only the challenge of giving birth, but also the challenges of motherhood. Like a first-class athlete, every woman needs to be prepared physically and mentally for the most challenging and rewarding project of her life.

When a mum-to-be comes to me for a postural assessment, I explain, simply and clearly, about these postural changes that her body will go through during the next nine months. I take a piece of paper and a pencil and I draw a few very simple pictures to show her these changes.

We discuss a suitable programme that will enable her not only to enjoy a healthy, pain-free pregnancy, but to face the challenge of delivery, and how to recover after childbirth. We also discuss how best to deal with the challenges of late nights, breastfeeding, and the fatigue that takes over. This is the time when a woman needs to be strong.

Both phases, PRE- and POST-natal, play an essential role in a woman's life and should be discussed and planned in detail.

I also explain:

How the body will have to recover after delivery to regain a proper postural alignment.

The necessity of strengthening the muscles that are being weakened by both pregnancy and delivery.

How to regain a good, healthy figure after the baby is born.

PRE-NATAL POSTURAL CHANGES

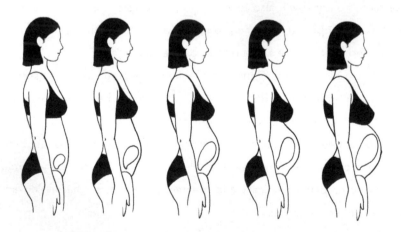

During pregnancy, the abdominal muscles will stretch and adjust to allow the baby to grow inside the womb. The natural corset that had been so tight and well laced up until now will have to be loosened in order to give the baby proper room to grow.

POSTURE

During pregnancy several changes occur; these natural changes will compromise your correct postural alignment.

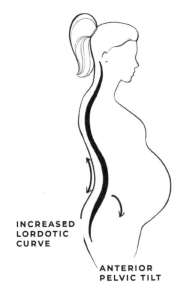

INCREASED LORDOTIC CURVE

ANTERIOR PELVIC TILT

This is the main cause of the lower back pain that plagues most pregnant women. Sometimes the compression on the lower vertebrae can cause the compression of the sciatic nerve. Some pregnant women will experience a very uncomfortable pain from the middle of the glutei down the back of the leg (Sciatica, see page 23).

CORE MUSCLES, AND DIASTASIS RECTI

The rectus abdominis muscles, commonly known as the "six-pack", will separate to allow the baby in the womb to grow. The tissue between this pair of muscles will be stretched more and more as the baby grows, and will lose its elasticity exponentially, especially if the woman has multiple children.

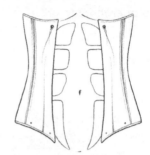

This separation can occur any time in the last half of the pregnancy but is most problematic after pregnancy, when the abdominal wall is weak and it will not go back to its ideal position, like a nice tight corset. The abdominal separation will reduce the strength of the abdominal wall and aggravate lower back pain and pelvic stability. Women expecting twins, especially very petite women, those with a pronounced lower back curve, or with poor abdominal muscle tone, are at increased risk.

Genetics also plays a big role. For some women, it is simply how their bodies respond to pregnancy. **This muscle separation is called diastasis.**

Exercising during pregnancy

I strongly advise pregnant women to exercise and be active. However, I recommend being very careful when choosing an appropriate exercise programme. Some of the common discomforts of pregnancy can be easily avoided by maintaining a proper postural alignment. An appropriate exercise programme can also play a significant role in easing your way to delivery. However, the programme has to take into consideration that ligaments during pregnancy will be loosened from the effect of the relaxin hormone, and inappropriate exercises might put excessive strain on the joints. **Check with your doctor or health care practitioner before starting any exercise programme.**

Pre-natal low-impact exercises are very effective, and I do advise them strongly. The Pilates Method is very safe both for pre- and post-natal phases. A suitable programme with the proper professional instructor and equipment will facilitate the exercises while maintaining you in the correct posture alignment. I have looked after mums-to-be until the day before they give birth, and they are in such wonderful shape, it's a pleasure to see them. They are happy, strong and pain-free, and, as they all tell me, they feel that the exercise programme I have created for them has facilitated the pregnancy. They will also tell me, a few days after delivery, how much the programme has helped them through the long and exhausting hours of delivery. They were aware of their breathing technique and used it to facilitate delivery. Both their core muscles and pelvic floor were well trained to be stronger and help them to push the baby without causing any strain in the lower back.

Recommended exercises during pregnancy

Rule No. 1: Always consult your doctor before starting any exercise programme while pregnant.

My recommendation is to avoid high impact exercises but, in general, to continue practising what you were practising before.

My preference goes to the Pilates Method with the use of equipment. It is low impact, intelligent, safe, and very effective both for pre- and post-natal stages. The Pilates Method will give you postural awareness, strengthen your core, and prepare you for the challenges of the long hours of delivery. **The Golden rule?** Choose a very reputable Pilates' centre (see my recommendations in Chapter 13, A PRACTICAL GUIDE FOR A CONTEMPORARY BODY) which offers specific pre- and post-natal programmes with qualified teachers.

Pre-natal yoga classes are also very good. My recommendation, again, is to make sure you are closely followed by an experienced teacher.

My Body ID Method will teach mums-to-be to practise the most suitable and safest exercises both for the well-being of the mum and the baby. It will also give the mum a great foundation and prepare her for the post-natal programme, and help speed up the time of recovery.

High impact exercises, gym, sports

In general, I do not recommend high impact exercises during pregnancy.

In my personal opinion I do not feel the gym is a suitable environment for a pre-natal programme. High impact exercises or exercises that require great physical efforts are not good during pregnancy. I would be wary also of trainers who do not have experience in pre- and post-natal programmes. This is a magical time to nurture your body and be in a safe and calm environment.

For sports, or other high-impact activities such as jogging or dancing, I only recommend them to a very experienced mover, an elite mover, an athlete or a professional dancer, and always under the doctor's recommendation. Even elite movers will probably have to modify their routines and avoid movements that can put their pregnancy at risk.

During my first pregnancy I personally enjoyed dancing very much until my big belly stopped allowing me to do so, in the 7th month. I was in Paris and my wonderful doctor told me that if dancing was good for me and made me so happy, it must have been good for my baby too. My body was very used to these daily dancing routines; I simply had to avoid high-impact exercises such as jumping and be sensible. I did stick to my barre for support and felt safe and happy. During my second pregnancy, this time with a history of a back injury and chronic back pain, I could not practise my dance routines and I only followed the Pilates Method. My second pregnancy was easy and pain-free, and my recovery was also very fast.

MY TIP

Be aware that your main priority when exercising during pregnancy is not stretching or increasing your flexibility (your relaxin hormone is already naturally doing so) but maintaining a healthy and strong posture.

POST-NATAL EXERCISE PROGRAMME

I insist that new mums take time at least twice a week for themselves, even though they are so taken with the new-born baby. The post-natal phase is crucial for the well-being of the mother and, in consequence, for the baby.

This is the time to:

1. *Restore your postural alignment, which will have been compromised during the 9 months of pregnancy;*

2. *Strengthen the core muscles that have been weakened by both pregnancy and delivery;*

3. *Tighten the pelvic floor muscles that have been strained during the delivery (both natural birth and C-section),*

4. *Take care of the diastasis, separation of the upper abdominal muscles.*

It is essential for every woman after delivery to follow a specific programme to restore the correct position of these abdominal muscles.

Most women complain after having had their baby that their tummy does not go back to being as flat as it was. This is because of the diastasis, the muscles' separation. This condition can be easily helped. A very specific programme devised by professionals specializing in post-natal care is the only way to go. Once you have closed the diastasis and restored the muscles' correct position it is safe to start exercising more normally again. And if you wish your natural corset to become tight again? What a question... of course you do... then these are your first steps to regaining a beautiful and healthy figure.

MY TIP

No exercise regime should be ever initiated without having done the necessary post-natal protocols.

I advise starting your post-natal exercise programme:

1 month after your natural delivery

2 months after a C-section

Once you have followed my post-natal recommendations, strengthened your body and restored your postural alignment, only at this point, and not before, will you be ready to go back to your favourite sport or exercise routines.

Easy and safe exercises to practise during your post-natal phase:

- *The Little Hen Laying the Egg, page 209*

- *The Elevator, page 211*

- *Breathing exercise with a towel, page 131*

- *Exercise with an apple, page 186*

MENOPAUSE

Menopause, a word that until quite recently was considered taboo.

No one talked about it. Mothers and grandmothers kept it quiet and secretive, away from us younger women, as if it was a kind of plague. Certainly, an embarrassment, as it was perceived as the end of our femininity.

As part of the baby boomer generation, I remember very clearly that my grandma and mamma never talked about menopause; actually, to be more precise never educated us girls about any hormonal changes such as puberty, or of course birth control; those things were never discussed. I have a vivid memory of myself as a young woman seeing my beautiful mamma suffering from terrible and debilitating migraines and not being able to understand where they were coming from. I felt so helpless and worried. Why was she unwell? It was simple, my mamma was going through menopause, but her malaise was never to be mentioned. So, I had to guess, and finally ended up believing that my 50s would signal the end of my life as a woman. How sad! I was 20 and had only 30 more years ahead of me.

It could not have been more different in my own experience. I was living in Singapore, and I was 45, quite early to start having menopause symptoms, and my GP doctor had totally dismissed the idea of it.

A year later, very lucky me, I was introduced by a friend to a renowned doctor who was visiting Singapore for an anti-ageing conference. This doctor is a world-leading pioneer and expert in menopause and bio-identical hormones. It was serendipity!

This doctor opened a new world to me, as well as to many women around the world. After we met, she had very kindly agreed to give a talk in my Singapore home to a group of women who were very keen on learning more about menopause and her avant-garde approach. It was 1999, and no one really organised a ladies' tea to talk about menopause. However, it was a great success, and the most powerful ladies of Singapore attended. During her presentation, I was transfixed, fascinated – I certainly wanted to learn more.

This was the beginning of a long-term friendship and mentorship, which brought me many years later to open my practice in her very successful clinic in London.

I had soon learned that my feeling a bit strange, even if too young, were indeed signs of an early menopause due to a previous thyroid operation done in London when I was 40. The removal of half of my thyroid, due to a benign lump, had messed up my hormonal balance and triggered early signs of menopause. My difficult divorce and personal grief were also an element of great stress that facilitated my hormonal imbalance.

The good news was, I was very well prepared! Under the expertise of this specialist, I glided through menopause like surfing on a big wave; I was in control and kept a skilful balance. Actually, I felt great, strong and empowered. I knew and felt that a new phase was starting for me at 50, and that it was not the end, but a new and exciting beginning, just as I say in the intro of my book. My 50s were challenging but magical years, and a new phase of my life had started.

Today talking about menopause, natural HRT, pelvic floor, and related issues is considered mainstream. Contemporary women have years beyond their 50s to feel sexy and beautiful and to look great. It is our right indeed.

So, what did I learn in my personal experience? First of all, maintaining a healthy hormonal balance was the key. I went under the professional guidance of my doctor and started taking natural HRT with bio-identical hormones.[3] A true-life changer. My healthy hormonal balance kept my MOJO going, my body strong and my mind clear, and supported me during the most painful and difficult time of my life, my divorce.

---

3 *Bioidentical hormones are hormone preparations made from plant sources (Mexican Yam) that are promoted as being similar or identical to human hormones. The chemical structure is 100% identical to the naturally occurring hormones produced by your body's own glands. Practitioners claim these hormones are a "natural" and safer alternative to standard HRT. Regarding Bio Identical Hormones therapy, there is a lot of literature available online, and I advise to do your own research; it will be very educational.*

I also observed at work and studied with great passion the physical and structural changes that happen during menopause:

- **Pelvic floor weakening**
- **Osteoporosis**
- **Weight gaining**
- **Pouch belly**

… and developed specific exercise programmes to help women. By the time I moved to a new and modern medical facility in Singapore, the prestigious Camden Medical Centre, I had developed an extensive movement and exercise programme for women's health.

Twenty years later women's health and its related issues are still a true passion; I collaborate with amazing doctors around the world in spreading the information to empower women of any age.

Menopause – it's not the end of our femininity but a new and exciting beginning!

THE IMPORTANCE OF THE PELVIC FLOOR MUSCLES IN MENOPAUSE

Pelvic floor muscles play a most important role in a woman's life and health.

The pelvic floor is made up of layers of muscles and tissue. These layers stretch like a hammock from the tailbone at the back to the pubic bone in front. They support the reproductive organs and the bladder.

Sadly, in this technological and medically advanced age, most women are not fully aware of the importance that these muscles play in the body.

People, and in particular women, should be more educated and informed about the importance of the PELVIC FLOOR MUSCLES and how, when they become weak, their posture can be affected.

I call the pelvic muscles the woman's fountain of youth; they are the anchor of our core muscles.

If the pelvic floor muscles are maintained strong and active, especially during and after menopause, we can enjoy a better posture, a better figure, feel more confident and finally avoid the annoying inconvenience of urinary incontinence.

Even after many years of experience, I am still amazed that today a large percentage of women are not aware of the important role that the pelvic floor muscles play in their lives, from a young woman experiencing her first pregnancy to a mature woman who faces the challenges of menopause.

It is so gratifying to see the look of enlightenment on the faces of women who have given birth, or women who have been suffering from different problems, such as urinary incontinence, uterine prolapse, or discomfort related to sexual activity, once they finally understand their problem. They have not been exercising the pelvic floor muscles.

In women these muscles are affected by hormonal fluctuations, pregnancies, the process of giving birth, and later, by the hormonal changes of menopause. As they are related to so many changes and challenges, these muscles are easily weakened and can become very unstable. Like every other muscle, pelvic floor muscles, in order to get stronger, need to be exercised.

EXERCISE IN MENOPAUSE

The right choice of exercise programme can be of great support during the time of menopause, both physically and mentally.

Be aware of not pushing your body too hard especially during this delicate hormonal transition. I repeat what I said in Chapter 3:

What happens when the female body is pushed too hard? It goes into adrenal stress and this creates havoc in that incredibly engineered but yet delicate hormonal balance; it's just like throwing an orchestra out of tune.

Quality of movement vs quantity is paramount; regular exercise and consistent routines, rather than sporadic visits to the gym that make you exhausted.

Choose an activity that will uplift your mood, it can be dancing, walking in nature, your favourite sport, yoga, Pilates, ideally two to three times per week and always accompanied by your 30- to 40-minute daily walk. That is your medicine…

Practise my pelvic floor exercises every day, just as you brush your teeth, it will take just a couple of minutes.

PHYSICAL CHALLENGES DURING MENOPAUSE

Osteoporosis

This is the loss of bone density, and it's common in menopause owing to a reduction in the female hormone oestrogen. Exercising is a MUST. To improve your bone density, you need to create an impact on your muscles. Unless you are an elite mover and sports professional, I advise going gently.

Not all women suffer from this condition. Women who belong to the Slim/Vata/Ectomorph Body Types are more susceptible due to their slim nature and lack of muscle tone. They need to work very consistently to maintain a healthy level of bone density and muscle tone.

I recommend:

- *A good brisk walk every day of a minimum of 30 minutes.*

- *Pilates with the Reformer machine. Exercises with the Pilates Reformer are ideal because of the machine's spring resistance. They are also safe because they support you in the correct posture alignment.*

- *Dancing, outdoor sports and activities and a suitable light gym programme under the guidance of an expert.*

Bladder incontinence

Practising pelvic floor exercises is the only and one rule.

Painful intercourse

Vaginal dryness due to a lack of oestrogen. Exercising your pelvic floor is essential.

Uterine prolapse

Uterine prolapse is when the uterus falls or slides from its normal position into the vaginal canal. It is more common in women who have had more than one vaginal birth. It is also related to weak pelvic floor muscles. High-impact exercises such as running, or exercises that require effort in pushing, are not recommended. A specific programme to strengthen the pelvic floor muscles is the priority.

How to get rid of the menopause belly?

This is probably the question I am most frequently asked in my practice by women in or after their 50s.

I call it the menopause pouch.

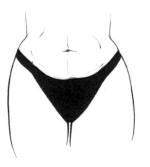

During menopause, weight gain is often associated with the accumulation of fat around the abdomen and internal organs. Our hormones also influence the fat distribution around our belly. The drop in oestrogen levels will create more cravings, lower our metabolic rate and increase our insulin resistance, meaning it becomes more difficult for our body to process sugars and other carbs.

Approaching our 50s can sometimes make us feel less active and motivated, with the consequence of losing muscle mass, and therefore slowing down our metabolism. Though the fluctuation of hormone levels and the reduction of the female hormones play a key role during this transition, a non-active lifestyle and an unsuitable diet can bear most of the responsibility for the weight gain during menopause. Balancing our hormonal levels and having a healthy and active lifestyle is the secret. The two go together!

The secret of maintaining an ageless body from your 50s on...

- *Practise a correct core strengthening exercise programme (see Chapter 9, THE CORE ISSUE).*

- *Combine aerobic activities like walking, swimming, bicycling, and playing outdoor sports with some strength and resistance training.*

- *The leaner your body is, the more calories your body will burn. The more muscle you have, the less fat, because muscle increases the number of calories you burn not just when exercising, but throughout the day, helping you to stay fit and slim.*

- *Reduce the amount of time you spend sitting down.*

- *Maintain a healthy and balanced diet.*

As I say in Chapter 3, FROM CAVE TO CUBICLE:

From the 50s on....

The Silver age and the Golden rule

This is the time of harvesting, the time of truth.

What we did or did not do looking after our body during the previous decades will manifest now...

The Golden rule:

NEVER STOP MOVING

Our contemporary body challenges.

- *Women are most challenged by menopause and hormonal changes.*

- *Our body goes through some unwanted but natural body changes.*

- *Osteoporosis.*

- *Urinary incontinence.*

- *Painful intercourse.*

- *Slower metabolism.*

- *As our weight goes up our confidence goes down.*

- *We do not recognise the woman trapped in that body...*

- *Panic! Mood swings, mental fog.*

- *We do not feel sexy.*

- *We think: I give up because I am old.*

We can't give up, EVER – a woman can be stunning and feel sexy way after her 50s; it is our right.

Solutions

- *Maintain a healthy hormonal balance.*

- *Keep moving and practising safe exercise programmes.*

- *Maintain a healthy diet, and healthy habits.*

- *Keep a positive attitude and move on with the times, live the present and do not stay stuck in the past. IT,S THE NOW that counts.*

- *Learn new things and new skills every day.*

- *Spend time with young people, they have a lot to teach us.*

- *Celebrate your ageless body and mind.*

If you stop, you become OLD!

To improve the strength of your pelvic floor muscles practise daily the following breathing exercises – I strongly advise these, especially for:

- **Weak pelvic muscles**
- **Post-natal women**
- **Uterus prolapse**
- **Lower back pain and lower back injuries**
- **Post-operation, C-section, or any lower abdominal operations**

THE LITTLE HEN LAYING THE EGG

I have created this pelvic floor breathing exercise to strengthen the pelvic floor muscles; it's easy, pain-free and you can practise it in the comfort of your home or even while you are working and sitting at your desk. This is an excellent exercise for these muscles. If practised regularly for a few minutes a day it will work miracles.

Sit comfortably and be aware of your sitting position. You should not be slouching, but sitting nice and tall, with a relaxed neck and shoulders. Try to use a good chair with straight back support or, even better, an ergonomic chair. Be aware of your sitting bones. Feel them by sitting on your hands. Feel those two bones a few inches apart, and make sure that your sitting weight is right on top of them.

Now imagine that you are a little hen who has just laid an egg.

Your egg is on the chair, underneath you. Visualize it.

Take your time and breathe gently and naturally, always counting 1... 2... 3... slowly.

Take a deep breath, and as you inhale 1... 2... 3... visualize the egg going slowly in and all the way up, floating from your vagina to inside your womb.

As you exhale gently and slowly 1... 2... 3... let the egg travel down from your womb through the vagina. Imagine it coming out. It would be the same sensation as removing a tampon.

Now the little hen changes her mind. She wants to bring the egg back up into her womb again.

Take a deep breath, and as you inhale 1... 2... 3... visualize the egg going slowly back in and all the way up floating from your vagina inside your womb.

Do not try to contract your abdominal muscles, do not force it.

Imagine holding the little egg inside your womb for a few seconds, and then as you exhale let it go slowly all the way down and out.

You should feel a clear sensation of tightening deep inside your pelvic floor muscles and your vagina.

It will help if you hold your hands on your abdomen so that, as you breathe in and out, you can clearly feel your navel going deeper and deeper towards your spine and your abdomen releasing towards your hands.

Do not force the movement; let it happen following your natural breathing pattern. **The movement should not be initiated by the contraction of your abdominal muscles, but from the activation of the pelvic floor muscles, from inside.**

Repeat it a few times a day; it will take only a couple of minutes.

THE ELEVATOR

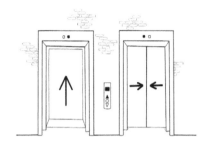

Another way to activate the pelvic floor

If you cannot relate to the Little Hen laying the egg, I use another visualization exercise called **The Elevator.** It is a personal choice. Some women prefer The Elevator breathing visualization to the previous one.

Again, sit comfortably. Be aware of your sitting bones. Feel them by sitting on your hands. Feel those two bones a few inches apart, and make sure that your sitting weight is right on top of them.

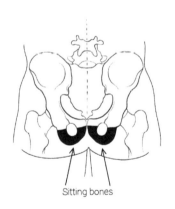

Sitting bones

Now visualize the sitting bones as the sliding doors of an elevator that operates internally from your sitting bones, ground floor, up to your waistline, the fifth floor.

Relax your neck and shoulders. Take a deep breath and, as you inhale, imagine that the sliding doors of the elevator, the sitting bones, are closing and your elevator is slowly going up. You will experience a sensation of tightening the pelvic floor muscles. Hold the elevator up for a few seconds at the fifth floor, exhale... and descend again to the ground floor, opening the sliding doors and releasing the pelvic floor muscles.

This visualization of the elevator should create a connection deep inside your pelvic muscles, a sensation of holding and release.

Again, this should not be initiated by an abdominal muscle contraction, or by contracting the glutes, but by a deep connection in your pelvic area.

You can practise both breathing exercises, The Little Hen and The Elevator, any time of the day. You can do it as you are sitting at your desk, while watching TV, or while you are stuck in traffic sitting in your car. Use the sitting time to add to your health and well-being. There is so much you can do while you are sitting. Both exercises have the same results, activating your pelvic floor muscles. Try both and see which one you relate to the most.

Remember breathing is one of the most powerful tools you have, and certainly your first step to a healthy new body.

SUSIE'S STORY

Susie came to see me for a postural assessment.

Her main concern was a uterine prolapse caused by the weakening of the pelvic floor muscles.

Susie looked sad, tired and out of shape. She described herself as being uncomfortable with her body and having lost her self-esteem.

She had changed from a healthy, body-conscious person to someone who didn't like what she had become but didn't know how to turn herself around.

She felt she had reached rock bottom.

Her doctor had advised her to follow an exercise programme to help her strengthen the pelvic floor muscles; however, the programme didn't seem to be effective.

When I asked Susie her age, she told me she had just turned 50. I felt sad, as I think this age should be celebrated as a second youthful cycle in a person's life. For Susie, this was definitely not the case.

Susie was a very shy person and did not talk very much. I did not want to intrude into the more private details of her life; however, I could see the sadness in her eyes.

I designed a special programme which took her uterine prolapse condition as a priority. We started with two private classes a week.

She needed to strengthen her pelvic muscles. She needed to focus on her core support. She also needed to exercise in a safe environment, and she needed an exercise programme to give her more stamina and more confidence.

She had shared with me that she felt very uncomfortable going to gyms or other places where she felt exposed and judged.

After a few months of private tuition, and with a dramatic improvement in her uterine prolapse condition, Susie was confident enough to join some mini-group Reformer Pilates classes.

She even convinced her husband to join the programme.

A few months after our initial sessions, I returned from a long summer break, during which time I had not seen Susie, and was stunned when I saw her.

She looked great, wearing a super fitted Lycra sports ensemble.

Her body was healthy, fit and toned. And best of all, when I looked into her eyes I could see a sparkle that had not been there before.

This was the sparkle of a woman who had regained her confidence. She radiated joy and beauty.

Here is her story in her own words:

In her own words

My name is Susie and I am 52 years old. Just when I thought I had lost the ability to enjoy life ever again, I found a way to recapture the wonderful feeling of youthful energy and the joy of being alive.

I used to live a very healthy life, but a few years ago two things happened to take the joy out of my world.

A very close friend was terminally ill and a close relative was extremely ill, and they lived very far apart. I was torn between the need to be supportive of my friend and the urgent need to be with my family. Although there was no real decision to be made, I was ravaged by feelings of despair because I couldn't be in two places at once. I decided to care for my relative who lived in another city and quite far from my home.

During those extremely difficult months, I had no time to think about myself. I was eating and sleeping irregularly, with little regard for my own health or nutrition. I was focused only on the recovery of this special person.

By the time I returned home I was physically and emotionally exhausted. When I looked at myself in the mirror, I hardly recognized myself.

I had put on a lot of weight. I hated my shape.

I felt fat and ugly. I didn't want to go out or be seen by anyone. My self-esteem plummeted. I felt anxious and no longer in control of my life.

My husband commented that I looked shorter. He was right. I did feel shorter, squatter. I felt as if the worries and difficulties I had been shouldering over the last months had crushed me.

Then, to top it off, after a routine check-up with the gynaecologist, my doctor informed me that I had a uterine prolapse, and I needed to do some special exercises to strengthen the pelvic floor muscles. That was the last straw. I did not know what to do or where to turn.

A dear friend and neighbour told me to GET OUT and DO SOMETHING. She suggested that I make an appointment to see Ivana Daniell.

I went to see Ivana for a postural assessment. The quiet, intimate environment of her studio was very reassuring.

She explained to me how I could strengthen the weak pelvic floor muscles and reassured me that in a few months it would all be fixed.

That very first day she taught me a simple breathing exercise that she called "the elevator". I have practised it every day since then.

After a thorough examination of my posture and discussing my daily habits and having also taken into consideration my feelings of inadequacy and low self-esteem, Ivana still seemed sure and confident about the programme she had chosen for me. She talked directly and honestly about the solutions.

After my first session, I left Ivana's studio with a sense of elation. I knew I was on the right path.

I started with a programme of two private classes per week and practising on a daily basis the simple exercises Ivana had given me as homework. After a few weeks I started to feel the changes. After a few months my posture had dramatically improved. I was walking tall again!

My core muscles were strong and tight. I had lost all the extra kilos. I had regained my best shape.

My prolapse was fixed. And most important of all, I had regained my confidence and self-esteem.

One year after my return from looking after my terminally ill friend, I was strolling in central London, having just completed my session at Ivana's studio when I saw a friend in the distance. I waved but she didn't respond. I kept waving at her, but she seemed to be ignoring me. Finally, I approached her. She was amazed. She hadn't recognized me. That day, I realized that I had truly recovered from a time of darkness in my life. I had regained my health and my youthful vigour.

On my 52nd birthday, my husband took me to a romantic dinner at my favourite restaurant. During the dinner, he looked at me and said, "That special person is back. The glow, the beauty, the body, the confidence and the special someone that was you, which I thought I had lost forever, is back in my life."

That was the best birthday present I have ever had!

CHAPTER 11

The HEALING POWER *of Movement*

JANE & FRANCESCA'S STORIES

A true inspiration

Never underestimate the healing power of movement. Maintaining your body moving efficiently is paramount, especially if you are challenged by an illness.

I would love to share with you readers the amazing and moving stories of two very special women who, through movement, decided to improve the quality of their life despite a very threatening illness. These stories are a true inspiration for everyone.

I dedicate this chapter to these wonderful and brave people who fought an illness with great courage, to Jane and Francesca, to my dearest friends Philip and Michael, and to all of you who are today struggling with similar conditions.

Thank you all to have put your trust in me, our shared healing journey has been a true inspiration and a learning experience.

These touching stories were written a few years ago when I worked in Singapore Camden Medical Centre. For those challenged by a neurological condition, one of the most important things is to maintain the body moving safely and intelligently; this will prevent and delay as much as possible the unavoidable deteriorations caused by these neurological conditions.

Singapore Camden Medical Centre 2005

Jane had been diagnosed with Multiple Sclerosis 13 years prior to her visit to my Singapore clinic. Her stage of the illness was what is medically called relapsing-remitting.

Multiple Sclerosis is a chronic inflammatory and degenerative condi-

tion where the body's own immune system attacks the myelin sheath that surrounds and protects the nerve cells. This process of demyelination affects the ability of nerves to conduct messages from the brain to the body. MS takes many forms and neurological symptoms may vary in severity from one person to another.

MS is often classified into three main types: relapsing-remitting, primary-progressive and secondary-progressive.

Relapsing-remitting MS is marked by relapses that last at least 24 hours. During a relapse, symptoms get worse. A relapse is then followed by a remission. During a remission, symptoms improve or completely go away.

Jane was 45 when she came to me, as a last resort; as she says, she was on her way to being bound to a wheelchair.

I did not want to take Jane as a client; I was very concerned. A few years earlier a desperate husband had brought me his wife, she was in a wheelchair, and she had Multiple Sclerosis. The poor woman could not move or function. I felt very sad and hopeless; I told the husband that there was nothing I could do at that stage. But that image of the woman hopelessly bound to a wheelchair and the desperate need for help from her husband had touched me profoundly.

When Jane approached me a couple of years later, I was still very concerned. I had never worked with MS patients and I had seen the devastating effects of that illness.

But what made me decide to undertake this challenge and work with Jane was that just at that time, one of my dearest friends in London, Philip, at the peak of his career, handsome and extremely fit, at 45, the same age as Jane, had been diagnosed with MS. The idea that my close friend might one day be unable to walk gave me the motivation to do something, I wanted to understand, I wanted to find a way to help him. I started studying the devastating effects of this terrible illness.

I called Jane and told her that though I did not know very much about MS I would love to work with her. Our journey had started!

Working with Jane during these intense years has been a marvellous experience and truly inspirational.

I have learned so much about MS while working with her. This experience has allowed me to work since with other people affected by the same condition. Most importantly of all, I have helped them during this challenging journey.

After the great result I had with Jane, quite a few people affected with MS have approached me.

Thanks to Jane, today many of my clients affected with neuromotor diseases have enjoyed the great results of learning and applying intelligent movement.

In her own words

Singapore, 2006

My name is Jane. I am 47 years old and today, like Ivana, I have never looked or felt so great. Thirteen years ago, I was diagnosed with Multiple Sclerosis which, at the time, seemed like a life sentence. It was a huge shock for my husband and our young family; we saw all our hopes and dreams for the future disappearing. I was desperately worried that their lives would be blighted by caring for an invalid.

When I first arrived in Singapore, I was struggling with typical MS challenges. My balance was already seriously impaired. I was considerably heavier than I am now, even though I was strictly following a diet prescribed for MS sufferers. I found negotiating steps increasingly difficult and had resorted to using an umbrella to help me to achieve better balance. I was clinging to handrails as if my life depended on them, which in reality it did, as stairs became more and more of a challenge.

I was facing a bleak future of deteriorating health and mobility.

Now I enjoy a wonderful life full of hope and adventure. I still have to face my challenges, but I am living my life exactly how I choose to live it, thanks to Ivana.

Five years ago, a very dear friend suggested that I consider going to Ivana's studio, situated in a well-renowned Medical Centre in Singapore where she herself was attending classes. She was so enthusiastic about Ivana that I was convinced I should at least have a look.

I think it was partly Ivana's immense kindness but, even more, her genuine desire to do more for me that kept me coming back. I was bowled over by the energy and focus she centred on me in her drive to make me better.

I discovered that, while physiotherapy sessions would leave me exhausted and dispirited, after the sessions with Ivana I felt uplifted. I had energy and I still felt energized the next day. It didn't take me long to realize which sessions were helping me. I dropped physiotherapy altogether and continued my classes with Ivana.

After my first session with her I felt cared about personally. Here was someone who really wanted to help me as a person, not as a client. It was heart-warming and refreshing.

Ivana gave me hope. She also gave me such positive feedback. I could feel the results immediately from the exercise regime that she personally devised for me.

My new regime with Ivana strengthened all the right muscles to give me back my balance. I could negotiate stairs. I began moving with confidence and, as a bonus, my physique improved.

I felt so uplifted. I knew I was improving. I could walk up and down stairs. I began to see the results, as well as feeling so much better. What was even more pleasing was that my husband and children, who had been so terribly worried, could see the difference. I came away from every session knowing I was better than the time before. I had a progressive degenerative disease, but I was gaining control, my health was improving, and I was feeling so much better.

Most of all, the gift that Ivana's programme has given me is a feeling of confidence that I had never had before. It is this new confidence that has changed my world.

What was so different about working with Ivana?

Ivana listened. She not only listened to me, but she also listened to my body. She worked tirelessly to understand my illness and she never gave up on me. She tailored every movement to address my specific needs. Her energy became my energy, and her joy at every small victory became my joy.

In the beginning, she took me very slowly through the movements. I tended to panic or freeze when I had to do something new. I was coming from a place of fear, pain and absolutely no confidence. Ivana took each movement and broke it down to its different components. Many of my muscles were damaged. With the programme Ivana tailored to my needs, these muscles were soon strengthened, and flexibility slowly returned.

One of the most important things I learnt was a totally new concept, the importance of the connection between my mind and muscles. Under her tutorage and encouraging guidance, I learnt to move muscles that I had never dreamed of moving again.

I cannot describe the elation I felt with the discovery of this lost connection when I could finally move with control the leg that had seemed to have gone to sleep forever.

The wonderful thing, the miracle of it all, is that I am living the life I choose to live. I am living a full, rich life that I would never have been able to have, if I hadn't met Ivana.

UK 2021

I was shocked to realise that it was fifteen years since I wrote the above piece for Ivana and much has changed in my life in the intervening time. We have left the sultry heat and urban sprawl of Singapore and returned to the fresh climate and gentle green hills of the English countryside. I am now 62 years old and have had MS for 30 of those years, almost half my life. Although it has moved from the relapsing-remitting phase into a secondary-progressive one, which is to be expected after this duration, I am happy to report that I am still able to walk independently and live a normal life. Something I would never have predicted 20 years ago when I first went to see Ivana.

I have kept my commitment to Intelligent Movement and to Pilates, because I know it keeps me mobile. I had found a Pilates studio near my new home almost before I had unpacked our belongings from Singapore! It has kept me moving and has brought the unexpected benefit of introducing me to a lovely group of ladies. During Covid the classes have moved to Zoom, and it has been such a joy to join our cheerful group every day. It has helped me both physically and mentally.

I often smile to myself when my new instructor compliments me on executing an exercise perfectly and think to myself "of course – I was taught by a master". More importantly, the fact that I can live a normal life and retain my independence is due to those long-ago sessions which taught me the incredible power of intelligent movement, and for that I owe a huge debt of gratitude to Ivana.

FRANCESCA'S STORY

I first met Francesca in Singapore, and she had been diagnosed with Parkinson's disease a few years earlier. Like Jane, she came to my studio after having tried everything with no results.

This time, a couple of years later, and far more familiar and experienced with neuro-motor diseases, I had no doubt I could help her.

The signs of the illness had started to show. Francesca's left arm was shaking badly, her neck and shoulders were in constant pain and very tense, her left shoulder was clearly out of alignment. There was a very visible hunch on her left side due to a pronounced bend in the spine. Her posture was severely threatened.

Francesca diligently started to see me twice a week. This time, thanks to my experience with MS patients, the results were almost immediate. Within three months the hump on her back started improving, she could easily control her movement, her posture had dramatically changed, she was no longer in pain and, as a bonus, just like Jane, she started showing an amazingly fit and beautiful figure.

Francesca was fascinated from the very first moment by my approach to exercise. She had a very deep understanding of the human body, as she had been working in the past in clinical therapeutic massage. She wanted to know more. I immediately suggested she apply for a Pilates Certification.

From the very first day, Francesca took her studies with great passion. In one year, she completed the most comprehensive International Pilates studies and decided to move back to the UK to open her own studio.

In her own words

Italy, 2020

My name is Francesca; I was diagnosed a few years ago with Parkinson's disease. Although I do sadly realize that I will always have Parkinson's disease, I have decided that I will never give in to it.

When I was first diagnosed with PD I started exploring all the different options and ways I could maintain control over my body, a body that soon would have been badly affected, weakened and shaken by the devastating effects of this terrible illness.

I was already experiencing some of the symptoms.

My left arm was shaking badly and, consequently, my left shoulder was in a very visible misalignment. To say it in simple words, I was starting to develop a very pronounced hunch.

My neck and shoulder were constantly in agonizing tension and pain.

My entire body was starting to feel weak and out of control.

I soon realized there were not so many options.

A few months before I had considered going to the gym, and I had tried some group Pilates classes. But the simple thought of attending any crowded classes with young, pretty, athletic bodies bending and bouncing around me totally put me off and made me feel extremely uncomfortable.

I needed a safe, secure and nurturing environment.

My own research into the illness had made me more determined than ever to avoid taking drugs that would have only had a temporary effect on the tremor. I needed a more movement-orientated approach. I knew I needed to do some form of exercise to maintain control and to stay strong and flexible. If I gave in the PD it would have taken his toll, and I realized that there would not have been a way back.

I had heard and read very good reviews about the Pilates Method. So, I started calling a number of places to inquire about clinical Pilates. I thought that doing Pilates under the guidance of a clinical therapist, or in a clinical environment, would have been a much safer option.

I wasn't getting very satisfactory responses until I called Ivana's studio.

I found her staff pleasant and encouraging and I was very reassured to hear that her studio was in a medical facility.

My first impression, when I entered the studio, was one of relief and anticipation. It was a bright, sunny room with an atmosphere of peace and harmony. A hint of tranquil music hung in the background. The studio was not full of young, energetic people moving strenuously to loud, upbeat music. At no time was I made to feel I was too old or too unfit.

I was greeted with a smile and within minutes I found myself talking to Ivana, relaxing, and sitting comfortably on a big pillow while sipping a cup of tea.

I truly appreciated how she listened to me without any judgement or discouragement.

During that very first session, Ivana not only did a very detailed analyses of my posture, literally from top to toe, but she also asked me very detailed questions about my lifestyle, my daily habits, my job and activities. She also asked me how the Illness had impacted my lifestyle, my job, and my movements. She talked about my movement personality. She explained how necessary it was for her to understand me, my daily habits, to know my needs in order to create an exercise programme that would be the most suited, not only for my physical needs, but also for my personality.

From that moment I was hooked!

We started working immediately, and in that first session Ivana introduced me to a new and fascinating world of intelligent exercises.

During the whole process Ivana was incredibly patient. She always answered all of my questions, she constantly reassured me saying that every exercise that she had chosen had a specific purpose, and she showed me how and why. I started to feel muscles I had not felt for years. Despite my initial difficulties Ivana was always positive and encouraging that this exercise regime would dramatically improve my posture, my twisted shoulder, and my tremor.

After only three months, I started to see big changes; I started to gain body awareness. My shoulder and my posture were dramatically improving. My neck and shoulder pain that I had had for the past few years was disappearing.

Ivana had taught me how to be in control of my movements. My tremor was not as visible as before.

Ivana was giving me, class after class, the emotional support I needed, so I felt safe and protected, but most of all she gave me the motivation to continue, to challenge my limitations, to excel and to fight despite the difficulties of my illness.

I had started out with two private lessons a week but now, a few months later, I had the confidence and the ability to participate in a group class.

I could finally mingle among the other students with great confidence. I looked fit, my body had regained the glory of the past years and my movements had nothing to suggest that I was suffering from Parkinson's disease.

Ivana has helped me so much. She has been a true inspiration; she has given me a feeling of confidence, of hope, and of total control over my body.

Today, years after my physical journey at her studio, when Ivana helped me and many others, I now want to do the same.

I want others to benefit from this research and practical experience.

Following Ivana's advice, I have studied to become a Pilates instructor.

I used to be a massage therapist, so I have a good background and knowledge of the human body.

I am now in my country, Italy, where I want specifically to cater to people with PD and help them the same way Ivana helped me. I want to give people hope; there is a lot to be done.

From my experience with Ivana, I have learnt that anything is possible. You can take control over your life, and over your own body.

An illness can be transformed from an impediment into a challenge and eventually into a new future and career.

If there is hope, there might be a solution, and I am glad I found it!

CHAPTER 12

INTELLIGENT MOVEMENT,
Intelligent Choices

In this chapter, I will introduce you to the methods that most represent the essence of Intelligent Movement, and I will provide you with a guide to recognizing and contacting reputable centres and professionals.

Now that you have gained a better understanding of your body and you have been educated on how to make the appropriate choices for your body, you need to know which methods are available and where to go.

Once you have started along the exciting path of your body self-awareness, I want to make sure that you keep to a healthy path, that you end up in the right hands, and with the right results.

So many people have started exercising with the best of intentions, but soon given up because they had chosen the wrong place, the wrong instructors and the wrong exercise regime.

WHAT IS INTELLIGENT MOVEMENT?

Is it a new technique?

Intelligent Movement is not a new technique. It is, rather, an intelligent way to approach exercise. It means learning to move in a more efficient way, with optimum results, and without any risk of injury. Intelligent Movement enhances the connection between body and mind and teaches you how to be more aware of your body and your movement patterns.

Intelligent Movement methods effortlessly create the right connection between your mind and your muscles and emphasizes the importance of good postural alignment.

Is Intelligent Movement a new REVOLUTIONARY concept of fitness?

Actually, Intelligent Movement is not such a new concept.

By the first half of the 20th century pioneers in movement such as Joseph Pilates, Moshé Feldenkrais, M. Alexander, and later, in the 80s and

90s, Juliu Horvath and Eric Franklin, had already fully developed their new and revolutionary methods.

They had created a new movement science.

But this new science was only available to a certain elite. And remained so for decades.

Originally the domain of professional dancers and sportspeople (elite movers) these methods have become more and more accessible to the general public during the past few years. They constitute the present and the future of exercise.

But what is so special about these techniques, and why should they work better than other forms of exercise?

It is because, when practised correctly and consistently, these methods will significantly enhance the following:

Movement awareness

Posture and structural alignment.

Muscle tone and strength without increasing bulk.

Core strength.

Coordination of movement.

Flexibility and range of motion.

Rehabilitation of certain injuries and physiological conditions.

An overall sense of well-being.

People of all ages, at all levels of fitness, from non-movers to athletes, may practise and benefit from these methods.

INTELLIGENT MOVEMENT METHODS

In this chapter I will not be talking about these exercise methods in great detail. There is an amazing variety of literature available on these subjects, and an infinite amount of information on the web.

I will be giving you, instead, a clear and concise explanation of what these methods are and how to access qualified instructors and reputable centres. Checklist below.

This book is a manual to guide you to the right choice of an exercise method for your personal optimum results. The following information is a brief introduction to people who have developed Intelligent Movement methods.

The Alexander Technique

The Alexander Technique was created by Australian-born Fredrick Matthias Alexander (1869-1955).

When laryngitis threatened his career as an actor, he began to notice that undue muscular tension was the cause of his vocal problem.

From his research and work on himself and others, he developed a method that encouraged the body to work more efficiently.

It is a very practical and gentle method for improving movement, coordination and body awareness. The Alexander Technique can help you to perform your everyday activities without unnecessary tension. You will learn to move in a natural, relaxed way.

An Alexander Technique teacher will help you to identify bad movement habits and help to re-educate you to more correct and efficient movement patterns.

This method is suitable for:

People who suffer from backache or stiff neck and shoulders.

People who feel uncomfortable when sitting at the computer for long periods of time.

People who are in post-rehabilitation from chronic injury.

People who are suffering from carpal tunnel syndrome.

Singers, musicians, actors, or elite movers such as dancers and athletes who wish to improve their performance.

For further information about the Alexander Technique and how to find a centre near you, go to:

www.alexandertechnique.com

The Pilates Method

The Pilates Method was created by German-born Joseph Pilates (1883-1967).

Joseph Pilates dedicated his entire life to the study of the human body, beginning with improving his own physical strength. He studied bodybuilding and yoga and by the age of 14 was fit enough to pose for anatomical charts. He ultimately devised a series of exercises and training techniques and engineered all the equipment.

His method, which he and his wife Clara originally called "Contrology", is related to encouraging the use of the mind to control muscles. It focuses attention on core postural muscles that help keep the human body balanced and provide support for the spine.

The Pilates Method is a low-impact exercise programme designed to stretch and strengthen muscles, release tension, improve posture and ease movements during daily activities, recreation and sports.

The Pilates Method focuses attention on core postural muscles that help keep the human body balanced and provide support for the spine.

Pilates is a very safe method, and it is suitable for a wide range of people regardless of age or condition, from teens to seniors.

In Joseph Pilates' own words:

The goal of Contrology (Pilates Method): "The attainment and maintenance of a uniformly developed body with a sound mind and the ability to perform life's daily activities with zest and ease."

"My work is 50 years ahead of its time." He was so totally right.

During the last two decades, Pilates has gained considerable popularity owing to celebrity endorsements. This method is not a passing trend. It is a very comprehensive discipline. The Pilates Method conditions the body from head to toe. It is not a quick fix. It requires practise and dedication; however, its results are worth the time and the effort. Here are some benefits.

- *Complements sports training.*

- *Develops functional fitness for daily life.*

- *Creates efficient patterns of movement, making the body less prone to injury.*

- *Develops deep abdominal muscles to support the core.*

- *Engages the mind and enhances body awareness.*

- *Enhances mobility, agility and stamina.*

- *Facilitates proper muscle recruiting to create efficient movement.*

- *Heightens neuromuscular coordination.*

- *Improves your appearance.*

- *Improves circulation.*

- *Improves strength, flexibility and balance.*

- *Increases joints' range of motion.*

- *Promotes recovery from strain or injury.*

- *Reduces stress and relieves tension.*

- *Relieves back pain and joint stress.*

- *Restores postural alignment.*

- *Tones and builds long, lean muscles without bulk.*

And again, in the words of Joseph Pilates: *"I must be right. Never an aspirin. Never injured a day in my life. The whole country, the whole world, should be doing my exercises. They'd be happier."* Joseph Pilates in 1965, age 86.

For more information about the Pilates Method, see:

https://www.pilatesmethodalliance.org/

There are so many Pilates companies that promote education.

When I started studying the Pilates Method in 1987 you could count them on one hand. Legendary teachers who had been Joseph Pilates' students were still alive, spreading the Method around the world. I was lucky enough to experience some of their teachings.

Their school is today called Classic Pilates, where all exercises are based strictly on the concepts as devised by the founder Joseph Pilates.

New generation Pilates or contemporary Pilates

A more contemporary approach has developed during the last two decades. In contemporary Pilates, a more modern approach is applied to the exercise concepts created by Joseph Pilates. Exercises used in the new generation Pilates are more influenced by biomechanics as well as physical therapy.

I would need pages and pages just to list the countless Pilates organizations in the world; here, I will just mention the largest ones which have representatives around the world and with whom I have worked personally.

They all offer high-quality educational programmes and very safe and good quality instruction. They have representatives worldwide and you simply need to contact them to check if there is a centre or teacher near you.

Balanced Body

https://www.pilates.com

Polestar Pilates

https://www.polestarpilates.com

Stott Pilates

https://www.merrithew.com

The Feldenkrais Method

The Feldenkrais Method was created by Ukrainian-born Moshé Feldenkrais (1904-1984).

He began working on himself to deal with a recurring knee injury. The method he developed is based on the principle of learning to move with less effort and more efficiency.

The Feldenkrais Method is suitable for anyone who wants to reconnect with their natural abilities to move. It can be applied to daily activities, from sitting more efficiently at the desk/computer to performing favourite activities and sport.

This method is suitable for:

People experiencing chronic or acute pain in the back, neck and shoulder, or in hips, legs or knees.

People who suffer from central nervous system conditions such as multiple sclerosis, cerebral palsy, and stroke.

Artists such as musicians and actors who wish to enhance their abilities and creativity.

Senior citizens who wish to maintain or regain their ability to move without strain or discomfort.

Any healthy individual who wishes to enhance his/her body movement awareness and improve his/her lifestyle.

Benefits:

This gentle method will improve your overall well-being.

It will increase your awareness of the connection between movement and thought.

It will help recovery from injuries and stress.

You will learn to move your body more efficiently.

For further information about the Feldenkrais method, and where to find a centre or instructor, go to:

www.feldenkrais.com

The Gyrotonic® Method

THE Gyrotonic® Method was created by Romanian-born Juliu Horvath, a former dancer and gymnast. He created this methodology after many years of intense study and thought.

This unique exercise system incorporates the movement principles of dance, gymnastics, tai chi and swimming. It is rapidly gaining recognition as a mainstream technique for body conditioning, sports-specific training and rehabilitation.

Gyrotonic® is a totally new exercise system that uses the Pulley Tower, a specifically designed machine, as the centrepiece of this methodology.

Gyrotonic® employs specific breathing patterns and circular movements under various forms of resistance. This is the basis for exercising the muscles and articulating the joints. Gyrotonic® simultaneously stretches and strengthens the body, increasing the range of motion and developing coordination.

Some benefits are:

* *Engages the mind and enhance body awareness.*

* *Enhances mobility, agility and stamina.*

- *Facilitates proper muscle recruiting to create efficient movement.*

- *Heightens neuromuscular coordination.*

- *Improves your appearance.*

- *Improves circulation.*

- *Improves strength, flexibility and balance.*

- *Increases joints' range of motion.*

- *Reduces stress and relieves tension.*

- *Relieves back pain and joint stress.*

- *Tones and builds long, lean muscles without bulk.*

For further information about the Gyrotonic® method and how to find a centre and qualified instructor please go to:

www.gyrotonic.com

The Fraklin Method

The Franklin Method was created by Swiss-born Eric Franklin, a dancer, movement educator, university lecturer and author.

After studying and training with some of the top movement specialists around the world, he created his own unique technique and founded the Franklin Method Institute in Switzerland. He offers workshops and training courses on topics covered in his books.

The Franklin Method teaches the practical elements of body design through imagery.

It has been adopted by movement professionals from ballet companies, art schools and music conservatories to athletes and practitioners of Pilates, yoga, fitness and physical therapy.

For further information go to:

www.franklin-method.com

Intelligent Yoga

There is so much information and literature about yoga.

There are so many different styles, techniques, I would need a volume just to list them all. Some are excellent, some are bad and, as in fitness generally, it's hard to understand the difference until you have experienced it. To keep you on the safe side I will only focus on Intelligent YOGA. Teachers who, like me, have strongly felt the necessity of guiding people towards the right and safe direction.

I advise you to check out *Intelligent Yoga* by Peter Blackaby:

www.intelligentyoga.co.uk

What is so special about these all of these Intelligent Movement techniques and why should they work better than other forms of exercise?

Firstly, they are all about finding the connection (the Lost Connection) between the body and the mind.

Secondly, you will learn about yourself and your body. You will develop a postural self-awareness that will enable you to better understand your body's strengths and weaknesses.

Thirdly, having developed that self-awareness and having found the lost connection, you will be ready to understand your body intelligence and make the right choices as to how to move efficiently and safely for your own unique body.

A PRACTICAL GUIDE FOR A
Contemporary Body

Movement is an essential part of our life. Our body is the vehicle of movement. We should be responsible and well informed when making choices concerning our body and suitable exercise programmes.

Some of the most important pieces of information that I give you in this book are intended not only to guide you step by step towards a better understanding of your body and to find out what is the most appropriate exercise programme for you, but also:

1. *How to find an appropriate and reputable centre*

2. *How to locate and choose the right professional or instructor in the area where you live.*

As I have mentioned many times in this book, quality of instruction and the right choice of an exercise programme is paramount to your well-being and to your transformation. Without it, you will be wasting your time and your money, and finally, you will end up with no results, possibly hurt, and most certainly frustrated and disappointed.

In this chapter, I will guide you step by step through this process, and if you follow my instructions, I am very confident you will have the results that you deserve and you that are hoping for.

THE MANUAL FOR YOUR CONTEMPORARY BODY

My guidelines regarding Intelligent Movement techniques should have given you a deeper understanding and a more precise idea of what is available today, outside the regular fitness, gym or yoga world.

By now you should be aware of:

1. *Your body type,*

2. *A suitable exercise regime for you,*

3. *A better understanding of what good posture is,*

4. *An understanding of the importance of core strength,*

5. *Your breathing patterns.*

Now it is time to MOVE, but where to GO?

My guidelines can apply to any kind of exercise; these are very safe guidelines applicable to any place you choose, from Pilates to yoga, from ballroom dancing to the gym. Quality of instruction is imperative; your first step is to do your research to find a reputable place.

This is one of the most important pieces of advice I can give you. It will save you from unwanted surprises, disappointments, and possible injury. Best of all, it will save you time and money.

Before you start any exercise programme you should make an appointment for a Postural Assessment.

It is the safest way to start your exercise programme. From this assessment, you will get a much clearer idea of your posture imbalances and you will be advised as to what kind of exercise regime is most suitable for you.

A suitable professional to do your postural assessment would be a good clinical therapist, an experienced Intelligent Movement instructor, or a Clinical Pilates instructor.

How to find the right professional for a Postural Assessment

1.   *Clinical practitioners, such as physiotherapists, osteopaths, or chiropractors are suitable to advise you on your posture and detect any misalignment. Not all practitioners are aware of, or informed about, specific exercise methods, and may not be able to guide you in the right direction. However, you will at least have a report and very specific recommendations about your posture to give to your future instructor.*

2.   *A clinical Movement Instructor, someone who has knowledge and qualifications in physiotherapy, osteopathy, or chiropractic, along with an Intelligent Movement Method, is probably the most suitable person to do your postural assessment, as these practitioners have both clinical experience and the right knowledge on how to apply it to movement programmes.*

3.   *The Ivana Daniell BODY ID Posture Assessment.*

You can have a BODY ID Posture Assessment in my clinic or you can book an online Posture Assessment.

www.ivanadaniell.com

Remember, the postural assessment is your safety net. You will have valuable information about your posture to pass to your future instructor and general guidelines of contraindications. If an instructor dismisses this information or tells you he/she does not need it, which I see often, my answer is: run away fast. This instructor is not capable of understanding the value of the Postural Assessment and will not understand your body and your personal needs.

If you have a medical condition, always ask your doctor to recommend a suitable professional and give you a medical report.

Personally, I do not accept clients who have medical conditions unless they have a recommendation and full report from their doctor or physician. This will also protect you, as not all people in the fitness/exercise field are aware of certain medical conditions and their contraindications. A serious instructor, if not comfortable with certain conditions and not qualified to deal with them, should be honest and say to the client that he is not in a position to look after him/her.

My clients have told me a number of horror stories where they have been enrolled at centres or with an inexperienced instructor interested only in taking their money. They did not have the right knowledge and qualifications to teach and/or help them. These clients continued the classes until, in frustration, they ended up leaving. They had lost time, effort, money, and trust.

Once you have your postural report, you will have a clearer idea of what kind of exercise regime is most suitable for you.

Now let's go to the next step.

How to find a qualified instructor and/or appropriate exercise centre?

There is only one rule:

Quality and Safety

Pilates, Gyrotonic®, yoga, gym, or other methods, my answer is always the same... quality of instruction.

Sadly, often, when something grows in popularity, quality is the first thing that will suffer.

Some of these methods, in particular, the Pilates Method, have become very popular and very trendy. As methods become popular a lot of centres or instructors will use them to attract customers. For this reason, you must be very careful about selecting the centre or the instructor. Be aware of:

Very poor-quality teaching and unqualified instructors. Instructors with inadequate qualifications from a non-recognized institution.

Unsafe facilities. Lack of knowledge, and lack of quality control from the establishment that is offering the classes.

Unfortunately, control in this area is very limited. Anybody can advertise for any kind of exercise classes. Some of these centres rely on the ignorance of the general public and the prolific misinformation that is disseminated. It is sad to say, but the people who own or run these establishments may not themselves be well informed about the programmes they are offering. I have seen so many fitness establishments and luxury wellness clubs hiring instructors with very poor qualifications. Their priority is in the luxury of the facilities and not on the quality of the instruction.

In the exercise world, there are no rules, it is the "Wild West", the "law of the jungle". You need to be well prepared with useful guidance for your journey into fitness.

It is not as it is in the medical or clinical environment, where there is proper control. We know we are protected by the regulations of reputable degrees when we visit a doctor or a clinical therapist and they display their qualifications on the wall in their practice, visible to all. In the exercise world, it is not so clear-cut. It is as important to know how to prepare for your venture into the world of movement as it is to prepare for the Wild West or the untamed jungle.

Until now people have relied on information they see online, on social media, or read in magazines – or a friend's recommendation. Some have been influenced by the latest trends, others have chosen an exercise pro-gramme because that particular facility was conveniently close to the office or home. Others simply chose an instructor because that instructor was so cute or so nice.

They do not do a proper "clinical research" as they should certainly do.

I believe the public has the right to be informed and educated to make intelligent and responsible choices, especially when it concerns their health and their body. This is why, today, most reputable organizations have an informative website with detailed information and a list of their recommended facilities and instructors, to guide you through this important process.

So next time you visit or call an exercise facility think twice about it and do a bit of investigation first. Don't hesitate to ask pertinent questions about their programmes and their instructors and what organizations they belong to.

HOW TO LOCATE A QUALIFIED EXERCISE CENTRE NEAR YOU

How and where to find the right professionals

Always do your research before you commit to anything.

If you log in to the official websites for Pilates, Gyrotonic®, Alexander Technique, the Feldenkrais Method, the Franklin Method and Intelligent Yoga you will be provided with step-by-step guidance on how to locate the centre or instructor of your choice near you. Please use it. This should always be your priority when you make your intelligent choice.

If you are searching in big cities such as London, NYC or Tokyo, you will have a wider choice. You can even find something near your office or where you live. But if you live outside a big city, or in a more isolated area, your chances are smaller, and you may have to consider travelling a bit to reach the centre of your choice. If you cannot find a centre near you, contact the representative of the organization; they will always assist and advise you.

Once you have located a centre make sure of the following:

Check the facility. Especially with Pilates and Gyrotonic® facilities there should be all the necessary equipment. It is important that you know what the appropriate equipment is.

A fully equipped Pilates' studio will have the following equipment:

The Pilates Reformer

The Trapeze bed or Cadillac

The Pilates Chair

And various small apparatus specifically used to practise the Pilates Method.

I recommend you visit **www.pilates.com** to see what a fully equipped Pilates' studio looks like.

Pilates with Machines versus Pilates Mat work (floor exercises)

Doing floor exercises will give you great benefits, but it will not be the same as exercising in a fully equipped studio. Many gyms or sports centres cannot offer a fully equipped Pilates' facility for two reasons.

1.   *The high cost of the equipment.*

2.   *They do not have the instructors qualified to use the equipment.*

There are many instructors qualified to do mat work only, but this it is not a comprehensive Pilates Method qualification.

Be wary of basing your decisions on such advice or information as, "I have friends who go to the gym and do Pilates on the exercise balls", or "I have a friend who knows an instructor that comes to their home and brings portable equipment. It is so convenient" or, even worse, "I do Pilates in my local gym, and it is so cheap. We do floor exercises and we do not need machines." None of this information is indicative of a safe situation, especially if you are suffering from a postural imbalance or recovering from an injury, or you are pregnant.

When looking for a proper Pilates facility, always check for the following:

Is the Pilates facility fully equipped with the appropriate Pilates equipment?

I have a very simple and straight answer when people argue with me on this particular point about why they should do Pilates with the machines when they can do it on the floor and use simple props like exercise balls or elastic bands. Have you ever seen a gym with no equipment? Have you ever seen a gym with just a few exercise balls, mats and elastic bands on the floor? I don't think so. Well, the same applies to a Pilates facility. Unqualified centres and instructors want you to believe that equipment specific to the Method is not necessary.

The Pilates equipment is necessary; it will facilitate your exercises and it will be much safer. The Pilates machines are designed with this specific purpose. In Joseph Pilates' own words:

"I invented all these machines. Began back in Germany, was there until 1925 [or was that 1923?], used to exercise rheumatic patients. I thought, why use my strength? So, I made a machine to do it for me. Look, you see it resists your movements in just the right way so those inner muscles really have to work against it. That way you can concentrate on movement. You must always do it slowly and smoothly. Then your whole body is in it."

Mat or floor Pilates exercises can be very effective when properly taught, but they are only a part of the full Method. Contrary to what people believe floor/mat Pilates exercises are far more challenging than the exercises practised on the machines, and very often not suitable for specific people, especially as classes are often conducted in large groups.

A Gyrotonic® METHOD centre will have the following equipment:

The Pulley Tower, the most popular equipment of the Gyrotonic® Method.

The Leg extension unit, the jumping stretching board, the Archway,

The Gyrotoner.

The Method offers also a programme without machines called Gyrokinesis.

I advise you to visit their official website to see what the machines look like.

SIZE OF THE CLASSES

In order to maintain quality Intelligent Movement, classes should always be held in small groups. If you have a specific requirement or an injury you should always ask for personal tuition.

I suggest that after you have had your postural assessment, you should do a minimum of four individual sessions of your chosen method. This will help you to better understand the principles of your chosen discipline. These one-to-one sessions will give you an opportunity to develop a personal interaction with your instructor and allow him or her to create and modify exercises to your personal requirements.

QUALITY OF INSTRUCTION

How do you find a good instructor, or, as I call it in my practice, a good **Movement Facilitator?** Just follow these basic rules:

The instructor needs to be fully qualified in that particular Method by a reputable international organization. Often the instructor will be listed on the official website of that particular Method, where you can check his/her credentials. Do not feel shy to ask the instructor about his/her qualifications. It is your right to know and to be in safe hands. Proper Intelligent

Methods instructors undergo a very serious intensive course of a minimum of one year's training. They also have to complete a practicum of supervised teaching with clients before they sit for their exams. This process may take another year.

In particular, Pilates' instructors specialize in different modules, which include: Mat Pilates exercises, Studio Pilates exercises, Reformer Pilates exercises, and Clinical Pilates exercises. So, when you choose your Pilates instructor, check his or her specific qualifications.

The same will apply for the other Intelligent Movement Methods.

I think it is fair to recognize the effort of these instructors who have undergone such long studies and training. They should be supported and respected, especially as there are those who have done only a short course and have very poor qualifications but apply for the same jobs.

I strongly believe that it should be the first responsibility of the management of the facility that offers the programmes to check their instructor's qualifications and make sure that their clients are in safe hands. Unfortunately, I see that it is not always the case, and that is why I want to guide you in one of the most important phases of your transformations.

If you are the pilot of your vehicle, the co-pilot has to be a perfect navigator and bring you to the right destination.

When looking for a personal instructor, remember, anyone can say they teach Pilates, yoga, or any other exercise technique. However, in the end, it is our personal responsibility to check the professionalism and the qualifications of the centre and the instructors. If you are to be putting your precious vehicle, your body, into the hands of a stranger, you must be sure you will be safely guided along the path of transformation.

My website will provide you with all the latest information and you will also find there a list of centres and professionals I personally recommend, together with details of how to contact them directly.

www.ivanadaniell.com

To better guide you, I have included here the stories of two wonderful teachers: Emilia and Rachele. They are both perfect examples of the kind of process a good teacher goes through to achieve the best qualifications, experience and knowledge.

Emilia has been my very first BODY ID Method representative. Today she runs a beautiful and successful studio in Milano. She is also a fully certified Pilates Instructor and a certified Gyrotonic® instructor. Emilia has been the most committed student and practitioner. When I met her a few years back she was a professional ballerina looking for a shift in her dancing career. I encouraged her to continue her education and specialize in Intelligent Movement methods because she had a natural talent in understanding movement and in communicating with people.

In the past few years, her skills have reached a very high quality of professionalism and I am very proud of having been her mentor and teacher. I wish there were more professionals with that knowledge and commitment. Emilia is doing a wonderful job in bringing movement awareness to the public and educating people in making intelligent choices when choosing an exercise programme.

Rachele joined my team later on and she is now working with me in my practice.

Ours is a true mission, and we hope that many more will join us to become a new generation of instructors or, I prefer to say, of Movement Facilitators.

EMILIA'S STORY

My name is Emilia, and I am a 30-year-old ex-ballet dancer. I studied classical ballet from when I was five years old in Italy. At 13 I continued my dance education at the Hamburg Ballet in Germany and subsequently at the Rambert School in London.

My journey as a dancer gave me a very good understanding of the way the body moves but, as you all know, we dancers have the tendency to push the body behind its limits, and often we end our careers with injuries.

This is exactly what happened to me and brought me to try the Pilates Method. I met Ivana during that time of my life; I was looking to deepen my studies in Movement. I had known Ivana for a while – our paths were linked by some interesting connections that came from being born in the same city. Ivana was living in London and, when I asked her advice about my future career, she suggested I join the best international educational programme in Pilates. Because Ivana was in London, we thought that the best choice would be to go and study there. I had spent some time in London while at the Rambert School, so London was for me a familiar place. Following Ivana's advice, I decided to take the most comprehensive Pilates Certification with Polestar Pilates.

While studying to become a certified Pilates instructor I also started studying with Ivana, to learn her innovative BODY ID Method. I immediately realized Ivana's unique and genius approach to Movement. I felt in syntony with her method and with my body. Ivana's method gave me a deeper *understanding of what I was studying for my Pilates certification and a different and much deeper understanding of the way we move and the way we teach movement. She taught me to become, in her own words, "An intelligent observer, to read people's bodies, and to listen to their stories". It was a revolution; I was now wearing a different pair of lenses. My focus was no longer on the performance of the exercise's routines but on the person. Our Body ID motto is "The exercise has to adapt to your body and not the body to the exercise". This says it all. It was a different connection and a different experience altogether. I completed my Pilates Certification successfully; but I continued my education with Ivana for more than a year.*

Then I finally felt confident enough to open my own studio. Ivana gave me the opportunity to be the very first representative of her Body ID Method and to become a Movement facilitator. In 2017 I opened my own studio in Milano, an elegant, cosy, intimate space where people can experience the joy and benefits of Intelligent Movement. My main mission is to educate people to be healthier and to better understand their body. Ivana and I continue our professional journey and cooperation, it's a never-ending learning experience and I wish to share it with the world.

RACHELE'S STORY

Memories of a Pilates teacher
– in her own words

My name is Rachele. I came to Pilates for the first time shortly after my third child was born. I had been running long distance for many years in between my pregnancies but, unfortunately, this time I was paying the price for the lack of core control and core strength due to my pregnancies. The third natural delivery was the last straw. The pain had become excruciating and did not allow me to sleep well and take care of my new-born baby and my two "very active boys" aged four and six years old.

My frequent visits to the physio only offered temporary relief and the pain was ebbing and waning depending on the day but was always a constant presence and worry in the back of my mind.

I had read about the benefits of the Pilates Method for lower back pain, and I decided to give it a go. In a couple of months, my dedication and consistency started paying off and I started feeling stronger and almost pain free. The relief was almost a gift, so much so that I decided to find out more about this method and joined a short, weekend-long Mat Pilates instructor course (Mat Pilates are exercises performed on the floor without the support of the Pilates equipment).

This course gave me just an introduction to the Method and some basic floor exercise routines.

Despite the fact that a weekend is far too short to learn the foundation of this Method I am grateful to the instructor who, for the very first time, gave me the confidence and trust to jump to the other side of the room and allowed me to teach my very first mat Pilates classes.

I was then aware that, if I wanted to progress, I needed to study the Pilates Method properly. I wanted to broaden my knowledge so, when the circumstances were right, I did a lot of research to find the best and most comprehensive course available to become a fully qualified Pilates' instructor. After having evaluated all the available options I chose a very reputable UK Pilates organization and signed up for an instructor course in London.

Different from so many other courses available, this one was very comprehensive and required almost full-time dedication for a year.

If people believe that to become a proper Pilates instructor will take a few weekends they are misinformed; if you want to become a proper Pilates professional it is a very serious commitment.

I started my course and studied diligently: theory, anatomy, physiotherapy lectures, 450 hours of observation, teaching practice, and especially training with one of the world's foremost experts in the Pilates Method. I also learnt how to use every single piece of Pilates equipment.

Once I completed my studies I started teaching group classes and private sessions in various clubs in London.

I knew how to teach hundreds of Pilates combinations, but somehow, something didn't feel right in my body and something was missing in my teaching. I was killing myself with endless routines of abs exercises, but my breathing felt shallow and constricted, while my muscles were tense and not supple. I was missing some form of harmony and suppleness in my movement patterns. I also felt the need to search deeper and understand more about the meaning of all these exercises I had learned during the course and how to convey them correctly to my clients. And then, I was blessed to meet Ivana Daniell.

We were both invited to a dinner party of a mutual friend... I was fascinated by her charismatic personality and, from the very first chat we had, I decided I would go and visit her in her London practice. I will never forget that day because, from a professional perspective, it changed the course of my career.

After a lovely chat, the very first thing she asked me to teach were some basic leg exercises on the Pilates Reformer which, for everyone who has ever stepped into a Pilates class, is the warmup and first basic movement you practise in a Pilates class. Well, let's just say Ivana deconstructed that single piece of movement and blew my mind by making me see it from a totally different light. It suddenly became the most sophisticated and intricate coordination of muscles, breathing, and a symphony of mechanisms involving the body as a whole.

I suddenly realised that though I felt I knew about anatomy, about exercise routines and movement choreography, until that very moment there had been a link missing without me being aware. I was not FEELING IT! I remember Ivana's words clearly, she said: "Rachele, this is not a performance, it is an experience, you have to FEEL IT!

It sounds so simple and obvious now but, at that time, it was a revelation. The difference it made, in every subsequent movement I learnt from her, was huge. It all made much more sense, and it shaped my way of teaching and the way I was able to cue to my clients and explain why those movements were necessary for them. The transformation I could achieve in their bodies was substantial, and the most gratifying achievement for a teacher.

When you experience the shift from moving just to follow an exercise routine or to burn calories to that sense of deep movement awareness and understanding, that is the real INTELLIGENT MOVEMENT.

I have been studying Ivana's Method for a while. Today, I feel different, I teach differently, with joy and depth, but most of all I am happy to see how people respond to it and how their bodies improve so quickly. Ivana taught me that teaching is about tuning in with people, in her own words "to become an intelligent observer". I love spreading this passion and being an advocate of Ivana's BODY ID Method to everyone.

CHAPTER 14

My
STORY

IVANOTTA LA BALLOTTA, IVANA THE LITTLE DANCER

From the moment I took my first step, according to my parents, I wanted to be a dancer, or as I used to say, a "prima ballerina".

My mother has always enjoyed telling me funny stories of how, from as young as two years old, I used to be constantly posing in front of mirrors in ballet poses, and how I would pirouette around the house during family gatherings and special family occasions, trying to attract the guests' attention with my little dancing shows. My parents often wondered how I could move in this way, and mimic ballet poses, as I had never seen a ballet performance. I guess dance was in my blood.

My sweet papa gave me the nickname "IVANOTTA LA BALLOTTA". This was his special endearment for me, a funny rhyme for 'Ivana the little dancer'.

Dancing, and expressing myself through movement, was simply part of my being. It was so natural to me.

From a very early age, I instinctively knew that movement, in any of its many forms (in my case, dancing), was a language, a way to express myself, my emotions and my joy.

By the time I was three, my mother could no longer cope with me pirouetting around the house, so she decided to take me to a proper ballet school. I was far too young, but she begged the ballet teacher to take me, saying that she would not regret it.

What a joy!!! Until today, I still remember with such detail the first time I entered the dance school: the smell of the ballet studio, the piano music in the background, the little girls in their black leotards and pink tights lined up at the ballet barre, and… of course… my very first little pink ballet slippers.

I was the youngest girl in the school, but it did not matter to me. I was a fish in the water. I was totally in my element.

My teacher adored me, and by the age of four I had reached my little ballerina dream. I was chosen to perform in the dance school performance, and my ultimate dream was going to become reality. Yes, I would wear my first pink tutu, and… at the thought, I still hold my breath… my first pair of pink satin pointe shoes.

At just four, I had reached heaven!!!!

This passion has never left me. I knew that day, what I wanted to do for the rest of my life.

I continued my dance education with a wonderful ballet master, Ludwig Durst. I was five and Maestro Durst's first student in Palermo, his first little ballerina. You can imagine the attention and the single-minded dedication I experienced from my wonderful maestro in that first year.

Very soon, word of this wonderful ballet master spread around, and my solo lessons in a tiny room in the basement of the theatre became classes in a rapidly growing group as we moved to a proper dance school with other students.

"Scuola di Danza del Maestro Durst"; I repeated that name, over and over, in my mind and aloud, with such pride, conviction, and passion. That was where Ivanotta la Ballotta belonged.

Maestro used to call me Ivanovna. He loved my name, and he told me I should, one day, be the star in the Bolshoi Theatre in Moscow. He never forgot that I was his first "Bambina". He always made me feel very special.

Then my life changed! The dark and dreary days of my new life engulfed me. From a life of light, love and dance, I was moved to a very strict and conservative Catholic school, where every expression of beauty was considered a sin and had to be repressed.

I hated my school; I was punished for being who I was, for being the little ballerina; for showing my dance moves to my friends; for expressing myself in graceful movements. I became a real rebel. I would dance in class, on the desks and, during recreation time, in the garden. I spent most of my junior years at school in the "Punishment Room", a horrible room, filled with scary, dead, stuffed animals. But for me, the nuns who ran the school were even scarier.

I simply hated my school.

One blessed relief from this life of doom and gloom was my afternoons at the dance school of Maestro Durst. There I found myself again, and I lost myself in the joy of dance. There I could, through dance and movement, express my joy, my sadness, my passion, and my feelings about myself. I existed. I was again Ivanotta la Ballotta.

I believed that my destiny was to become, as maestro always said, a prima ballerina.

Then my dreams were shattered. In a very conservative Sicily of the 60s, being a dancer, even a classical one, was not an appropriate choice for a girl in my family. My father had different plans. It had been decided long before. I had to follow the "family tradition", and become a lawyer like my dad, and my grandpa, and my great grandpa. I was the firstborn, and I had no choice. Imagine my distress. I was to go from a Bolshoi Swan Lake ballerina to the Court of Palermo, most probably having to defend a local mafioso. What destiny!

I was 10 when my mother told Maestro Durst that I had a different destiny planned for me and, without warning, she withdrew me from the dance school.

I was totally devastated. Maestro had chosen me that very year to be the principal dancer of the dance school performance. It was my first important solo. It was my first prima ballerina role. I had rehearsed my part for months. Maestro wanted me to shine, to be the star.

I never did perform that dance.

That tragic event did not kill my youthful, dancer spirit; after all, it was the 60s, the time of the Beatles, the beginning of an exciting new era. Ivanotta la Ballotta did not die. She continued living and surviving through the YEAH, YEAH, YEAH times to become the star of the pre-teen party scene, shaking and moving to the rhythm of the Beatles' music.

You can take the dancer out of the ballet school, but you cannot take the dance out of the dancer.

Eventually, after a few years of begging and pleading, I was allowed to return to Maestro Durst's ballet school but, as I had promised my parents, only as a hobby.

My future law education had to be the priority, and so it was until I was 21.

Unfortunately, for a career as a prima ballerina, it was too late for me. By missing those formative years, I never did recapture that which all those hours of training gave my ballet classmates. A few of them went on to be well-reputed prima ballerinas in major European theatres, leaving me with the devastating realization that I could never recapture those lost years.

At 19, to the great joy and pride of my father, I entered the Law school of the University of Palermo.

I did my best. I studied there for three years. I worked diligently to please my father.

But deep inside me, I knew that this was not my destiny. I became more and more frustrated; I felt trapped and repressed and wanted so badly to escape a destiny that I had not chosen. At 22, I begged my father to send me to England for one month to learn English.

"If I cannot learn properly the language of dance, at least let me learn a language that could be useful for my future as a lawyer," I begged my papa. Though he talked long and hard trying to convince me that the only language worth knowing for my future law career was Latin (which I had already been studying for eight years), he finally agreed to send me to Oxford to study English in an academy for foreign students. That very first trip on my own was the beginning of my new life, of my true destiny.

That was the first step that eventually brought me back to my dancing world.

There, in my 20s, I had the power of choice. I did not stay in England for a month, but for two years. Goodbye, Law school! I never returned to it.

Ivanotta la Ballotta, the little dancing rebel, was reborn, no longer a ballerina with pink satin shoes and a pink tutu, but this time as someone totally in control of how I moved and where I moved.

I wanted to explore the beauty of movement; I wanted to have a different understanding of dancing.

I started studying modern dance, and in the early 80s, with my dear friend and great artist, Rodolfo Diaz, from Buenos Aires, founded the first Modern Dance centre in Sicily.

Yes, I went back to my hometown, but not for long. The dance itch was stronger than ever, and though the school was a big success, after two years, I found myself following my dream to Paris.

I wanted to live in the Arts. I wanted to live and dance. Paris, "la Ville Lumière", the city of light, was the perfect place.

With a courage that I didn't even recognize as courage, I drove my old, red Renault 4 car packed with my most precious belongings from Palermo to Paris to start a new life adventure.

I will never forget those intense, beautiful years. I was living in Paris during some of the most incredible years of my life. I was living the ultimate Bohemian life.

I stayed in Paris for five years, developing my professional dancing and teaching career. I rubbed shoulders with the most amazing artists. I learned from the best teachers. I danced for prestigious companies. I continued and perfected my teaching career and taught in a number of prestigious schools.

There my son Vinci was born, and I become a mother.

After five intense years in Paris, I moved to London and started a new chapter of my life.

In London I returned to my first passion, ballet.

Through my dancing colleagues, I heard of a very prestigious school in London, "The Laban Centre". In my mid-30s and searching for direction in my career, this was exactly what I was looking for.

The school had a special post-graduate course for Movement, Choreography, Teaching Studies and Pilates. I wanted to add depth to my knowledge of Movement.

By the time I graduated from the Laban Centre, I had already made my choice. I wanted to explore more the healing side of movement. I wanted to help dancers and movers who, like me, had suffered a severe, career-threatening injury. A broken foot while pirouetting and a very bad fall on my back during a dance rehearsal.

I focused my studies on the Pilates Method, at that time unknown to the general public.

And I become a mother again; I was gifted with another beautiful boy, Christian.

I had a great life in London, a perfect home, two beautiful children, and I had successfully completed my dancing career and had moved on to the rewarding but more therapeutic side of dance.

Then once again, the Bell of Change tolled loud and clear. This time, when I thought that everything in my London life was just PERFECT, my husband announced that we were moving to Singapore.

Again, a new life and more unexpected times were waiting for me.

From the moment I moved to Singapore, I realized that the expatriate wife's lifestyle was something that did not suit me.

My husband kept telling me to enjoy it, to take it easy; "You don't need to work or worry about anything."

I think he felt a bit guilty that he had uprooted me from my PERFECT LIFE in London, and truly wanted me to enjoy my time in Singapore.

But Ivanotta la Ballotta, the dream, the vision, the mission, was always there. I had to be doing. After a few lunches at the local Expatriate Club, I felt I was going to go insane if I didn't have something more constructive to do.

We had moved into a beautiful colonial house in the middle of Singapore, on Goodwood Hill. These homes are called "black and white" houses because of the paintwork and resemblance to the Tudor style homes in England.

The house was surrounded by a hectare of lush tropical garden. We were in a real jungle, a true Eden, with colourful tropical birds, beautiful trees and flowers, a visiting monkey called George, and all kinds of small reptiles and spitting cobras, one of which eventually almost blinded our poor dog, Jordan.

It was there, in the middle of my tropical Eden, that I created my Pilates studio, which used to be the horse stalls, during the glory days of colonial Singapore, and more recently, the office of the previous tenant.

In this glorious jungle setting the very first Pilates Studio in Singapore and southeast Asia was born. It was 1998. Pilates did not exist in Singapore, or anywhere else in southeast Asia.

I had brought with me from London a "Pilates Reformer", the most popular machine among the equipment designed by Joseph Pilates.

Of course, my first idea was to teach professional dancers. In London,

I had worked with artists and injured dancers. I wanted to do the same in Singapore. It was my area of expertise.

One day, my new neighbour, Alice, asked me about the Pilates Method. I told her I was very happy to show her my new studio and to give her a trial class.

Alice became the first client of Ivana Daniell Studio.

A few days later, some friends of Alice called me. They had heard of this Pilates Method in the United States and London. They wanted to try it too.

Within a month I was fully booked.

Believe it or not, some of these original clients are still very dear friends, and still in touch with me today. They diligently followed me when I moved to bigger premises, and some even come and see me now that I am in England.

They say luck is nothing but... "Being in the right place... at the right time... doing the right thing."

My small Pilates studio became a reputable, successful establishment. Within a few months, I was interviewed by several prestigious magazines and newspapers. I was interviewed on TV, talking about Pilates and my studio. Everybody wanted to do Pilates. Suddenly I had a waiting list.

At that time, I heard of a new method called Gyrotonic®, invented by a Rumanian ex-dancer called Juliu Horvath.

I contacted the Gyrotonic® organization in the United States, and, with my luck running true, they put me in touch with their representative in Hong Kong.

Dawnna Waybourne had taken Pilates and Gyrotonic® to Hong Kong. She was a Royal Ballet graduate. The very talented Dawnna was the one who introduced me to the fascinating world of Intelligent Movement.

Thanks to Dawnna, who still represents Polestar Pilates in Asia, I met both the founder of Polestar Pilates, Brent Anderson, and the founder of the Gyrotonic® System, Juliu Horvath. I also had the honour of studying under their personal tuition.

It was an incredibly exciting time. I decided again to become a student. This time there would be no dancing, but my interest would be focused on a deeper understanding of the true HEALING POWER OF MOVEMENT.

Unfortunately, during this most exciting time in my career, my private life was disintegrating. In the midst of so much professional success, I found myself struggling to come to terms with a very painful and bitter divorce, which left me emotionally shattered.

I had left my perfect life in London, my perfect home, my friends and the close proximity of my family who lived in Italy, just two hours away by plane, to come to a foreign country, where I was new to the culture and laws of the country. I was alone, facing the challenges of a difficult divorce.

Yes, finally, I had entered the world of the law court and was working within the laws of the country, sadly not as a lawyer but as the respondent to a very painful and difficult dispute. In the daily swirl of meetings with lawyers, dealing with endless reams of divorce papers, and attending weekly court appointments, I struggled to come to terms with a legal system totally different from the one I had studied in Italy.

My tough years of "survival" in Paris came in very handy, although, having become accustomed to a comfortable lifestyle, being thrown into the harsh reality of a very painful and complicated break-up was very difficult. I had to roll up my sleeves and once again face some unpleasant facts of life.

My work was my safety net, my survival, my comfort, my moment of peace, my safe haven. I don't know how I would have survived those difficult years without it.

My children were my "raison d' être". My clients and my work became my mission and my passion.

The more difficulties I encountered in my personal life, the more motivated I became to succeed in my work, and the more I connected to people with whom I worked.

It was as if life had sent me a big challenge and had tossed me on to a rollercoaster which I had to learn to ride before I was thrown off.

And what a ride! Believe me! Many times, I felt I was being flung out, barely hanging on by my fingertips, fearful, hurt, bruised and exhausted. But I always managed to climb back in, determined to finish the ride. It took me a few years, many bruises, and a few broken bones, but eventually, I learned to control the ups and downs of the ride. I took full control of my life.

My little studio in the middle of a beautiful tropical garden moved to a prestigious medical centre.

A new, modern hospital facility had opened in Singapore, the "Camden Medical Centre" and I was invited to be one of the residents. That was 2001.

I spent 10 amazing years in the Camden hospital. My centre grew as the most established Pilates and exercise rehabilitation studio in southeast Asia. I gave many young professionals from all over the world the opportunity to work in my centre. Singapore had become my home, and my children had a safe and exciting upbringing.

My Pilates studio became more and more the centre of my own Method and in 2005 became LIFE in MOVEMENT. I was interested in exploring further the clinical side of movement. Working in a hospital was just perfect for me. I had the opportunity of working with incredible doctors from all over the world. My curious nature pushed me to study more and more and go deeper into the understanding of the human body.

In 2007 an amazing opportunity was presented to me. The most exclusive hotel company in the world, Aman Resorts, offered me a position as a consultant, to create and develop Aman Pilates Studios all around the world. What an amazing experience, and what a journey! I travelled for those 10 magical years from continent to continent, from China to the canyons of the US, from tropical paradises to Japan, and spent a lot of time in one of my favourite places in the world, Greece.

I was still living in Singapore; my Life in Movement centre was now a very big establishment. My oldest son, Vinci, was studying in Australia, my youngest Chris was in boarding school in the US. My life was divided between being a mother, a businesswoman, and a consultant to Aman Resorts. I was travelling so much that, one day while visiting my son Chris in Boston, I woke up and, for a moment, I did not remember which country I was in. I thought, "That's *it! This is too much…*"

The itch was back again. I needed a change, I needed to be back home, and home for me was only one place. London.

Life is always full of surprises; in 2009 while in London on my way to South America, a doctor friend asked me to see her VIP client who had suffered an injury.

That changed my life!

In 2011 I moved back to London with my older son, Vinci. Chris was studying on the east coast of the US, so it was not so bad to fly from London, much easier than travelling from Asia.

I began another chapter of my life. I was already in my late 50s and ready to start all over again.

Leaving Singapore was traumatic. It had been my home for 14 years. I had met the most incredible people and had very special friends that had become like my family. I was not prepared for the big change of living in Europe again. Though I still worked for Aman Resorts and had the oppor-tunity to travel to Asia for work, finding myself as a single career woman in a big city like London was challenging, to say the least. My support bubble of Singapore had vanished. My old London friends from the time of my marriage did not accept me back as I was "single" and, in their own words, I "did not fit" in their married couple social circle. I was sad and hurt. I had to restart my career from scratch; no one knew my work here. I had to face a very harsh reality. I had to prove myself as a professional, and I had to work very hard – the competition was fierce. I opened my own Posture Clinic in October 2011. This time the formula "the right time, in the right place, with the right product" DID NOT WORK!

Something was missing. Europe is very different from Asia. In a multi-cultural and fast-growing city like Singapore anything innovative is accepted and celebrated. In London it is quite the opposite, so bringing a new concept and a new method can be quite a challenge. To be honest, when I look back, those were very tough years. My main consolation was my children. Vinci, my oldest son, was working in London, and he had met the love of his life. Chris was at university near NYC. I flew to see him as much as I could. My other consolation was my wonderful job with Aman Resorts. I still travelled extensively. Sadly, the dream was soon to be over after 10 years of working for them. The hotel company was sold to a new Russian owner who decided to bring changes and new people. My last project was in Tokyo, then, after 10 years with Aman Resorts, I found myself facing harsh reality. I told myself, "You are now in London for the foreseeable future, and you'd better make it happen! My dedication to my work and my passion were almost the only things I had left, as well as, of course, the support of my incredible clients, who believed in me and trusted me. Another difficult ride, but my maturity and wisdom were my anchor. With great determination and patience, I rebuilt in London what I thought I had lost. This time with greater knowledge and depth, I was again in full charge of my destiny. This was the beginning of my BODY ID Method.

A new and exciting phase of my life was about to start, and I had just turned 60.

I dove into my work to develop my BODY ID Method, I started writing, studying, and meeting new and exciting people and professionals. And my small Posture Clinic grew more and more.

Now, years later, with a lifetime of study, experiences, and life changes behind me, I am where I am today, happy and fulfilled. Never, in all that time, during all the ups and downs, or while facing the challenges that life has a habit of throwing our way... Never once have I been distracted from my mission.

I have kept my word!

I have helped hundreds of people. My wonderful clients, who have been my teachers, my inspiration, and my greatest supporters – I have learned so much from them, listening to and sharing their stories, their aches and pains, observing, studying and listening to their bodies.

I have experienced the joy and the blessing of being told:

"Thank you, Ivana. You have helped me. You have changed my life."

"I feel great, I have no more pain."

"I love my new shape and feel so confident."

"I feel 10 years younger."

"My husband is so happy. He tells me I am so beautiful!"

I cherished these words. What joy!

I am where I wish to be, I am a woman, a mother, a grandmother, and a therapist.

My riches? A healthy mind in a healthy body.

Yes, I am proud to tell the world my age and I look forward to new and exciting times ahead of me.

Now it's time for you to MOVE...

Enjoy the ride and your future life as an Intelligent Mover.

Wishing you Love and Health,

Ivana

About the Author

Ivana Daniell, Italian born, is a graduate of the renowned Laban Centre in London, and the founder and director of Ivana Daniell BODY ID.

Having dealt with a bad back injury in the past, Ivana's main motivation has become to make people feel better. Over the past 30 years, she has looked after people from all over the world, including royalty, athletes, film and music personalities, and anyone who wishes to move more intelligently. Her clients have become a constant source of inspiration.

Her innovative BODY ID method is based on many years of professional experience in dance, Intelligent Movement, Movement Therapy, and observations of the human body, and is proven to be effective for long-term relief from chronic back pain, safer alternative programmes to physical fitness and the prevention of muscular-skeletal damage.

Ivana pioneered her revolutionary approach by applying a holistic technique that encompasses a person's lifestyle, physical characteristics, and mindful well-being.

She has collaborated with renowned doctors and clinics, from London to Singapore, even introducing the Pilates Method and other intelligent movement methods to Singapore and southeast Asia in 1998.

Ivana now runs her posture and movement re-education clinic in the renowned Harley Street medical hub of London.

Connect with Ivana

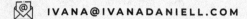 IVANA@IVANADANIELL.COM

 WWW.IVANADANIELL.COM

 @IVANADANIELLOFFICIAL

Lightning Source UK Ltd.
Milton Keynes UK
UKHW020855280222
399331UK00009B/505